NEW
BOOK

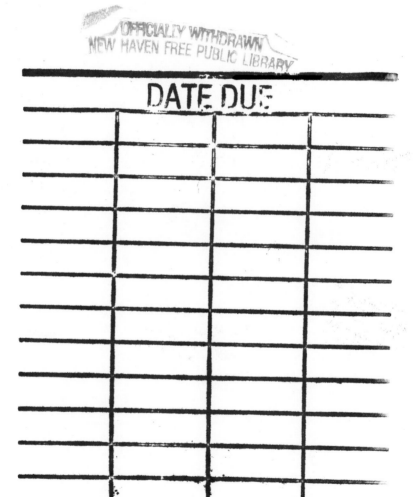

DATE DUE

D1413667

The First 12 Months of Motherhood

The First 12 Months
of Motherhood

by
Susan Hassebrock
Foreword by Susan Blase, M.D.

Lowell House
Los Angeles

Contemporary Books
Chicago

Library of Congress Cataloging-in-Publication Data

Hassebrock, Susan.
    The first 12 months of motherhood / by Susan Hassebrock.
       p.   cm.
    Includes index.
    ISBN 1-56565-449-8
      1. Mothers—United States.   2. Motherhood—United States.
   3. Mother and infant—United States.   4. Infants—Care—United
States.   I. Title.
HQ759.H34 1996
306.874'3—dc20   96-6096
                                                       CIP

Requests for such permissions should be addressed to:
Lowell House
2029 Century Park East, Suite 3290
Los Angeles, CA 90067

Lowell House books can be purchased at special discounts when ordered in bulk for premiums and special sales. Contact Department JH at the address above.

Publisher: Jack Artenstein
General Manager, Lowell House Adult: Bud Sperry
Managing Editor: Maria Magallanes
Text design: Laurie Young

Manufactured in the Unites States of America
10 9 8 7 6 5 4 3 2 1

This book is dedicated to my son, Jesse, the greatest gift I have ever been given, and to my husband, Harold, with whom I lovingly share this treasure.

Acknowledgments

I cannot name all of the people who helped me in some way, great or small, to complete this book. In general, I want to thank the friends who tolerated my absenteeism during the long months of writing and editing, and the family members who put up with my obsession.

My gratitude goes especially to the mothers who shared their experiences with me—Anne, Jennifer, Lisa, Tammy, Karen, Kelli, Laura, Tracy, Chalene, Gayle, Shelley, Stacey, Kimberly, Marsha, Patti, Michele, and countless other women I talked with in elevators, waiting rooms and grocery-store checkout lines.

I am also grateful for the help provided by the medical professionals and other experts I consulted during the writing of this book, particularly Dr. Susan Blase, who helped me bring a healthy baby into this world, and Dr. Sheila Ponzio, who helps me keep him that way.

Thanks also to Claudia Suzanne, a fellow writer who inspired me to write this book and never hesitated to suggest I "lose" the parts which were repetitive, boring or obviously written while suffering from sleep deprivation.

Contents

Foreword

As a first-time mother and a physician, I was very excited to be asked to review a book addressing the changes a woman goes through during her first year of motherhood.

This first critical year is filled with excitement, joy, exhaustion, and terror—sometimes all in the same day. Following one mother's personal journey is an excellent way to address the physical and emotional changes experienced during the first, life-altering twelve months of her child's life.

One of the things that impressed me the most was the wide range of viewpoints presented on the subject, from physicians to stay-at-home mothers and working moms. I enjoyed reading about other women's views of the first year and found them not too far from my own experience.

This is the first book I have had the pleasure of reading which gives a new mother good information about what to expect from and of herself in the first year.

Because the book addresses the various subjects in chronological order, month by month, it is easy to see that motherhood does get better with time. As her experience and confidence grows, so does a new mother's ability to cope with the myriad demands now being placed upon her. This book demonstrates how a woman's life is dramatically changed by the birth of a child and how she gradually learns to assume the wearing of so many hats—that of mother, wife, friend, and employee—all at one time.

The First 12 Months of Motherhood closely examines the infinite emotional dilemmas a new mother must face, from feelings of guilt and inadequacy to postpartum depression and weight loss.

As a physician, I was already aware of the physiological aspects of the postpartum experience, but it was nice to hear from other "real" mothers that these physical and emotional changes do take place as described in medical books.

Every novice mother has questions about her new role, and if she has few resources from which to obtain information, the first year is made much more difficult. She cannot always rely on her mother, friends, or health professionals to help her get through the long days and even longer nights. She may feel frighteningly alone in this endeavor, but this book offers reassurance that her feelings and reactions are normal and that other women are experiencing the same joys and struggles in much the same way.

The First 12 Months of Motherhood is easy and enjoyable to read and will be very useful to first-time moms prior to the birth of their child.

SUSAN BLASE, M.D.

Introduction

I was not going to go gently into the oblivion of motherhood. I was happy about the coming birth of my first child, yet I vowed not to surrender my independence or my freedom. But as I looked into my son's eyes for that very first time, I knew I would not only give up my liberty, I would relinquish my very life for him.

Sound a bit melodramatic? Wait your turn. In that first moment of motherhood, you will begin to experience emotions you never dreamed would be your own. Love, wonder, awe, fierce protectiveness, and absolute fear washed over me like warm water when they laid Jesse in my arms for the first time. I could feel myself being swept away by this raging river of emotions, each one fighting for top billing. It was both exhilarating and terrifying—I loved the ride, but I knew I was in over my head and not sure I could swim.

The umbilical cord is cut only a few moments after the baby is born, yet that physical connection is never completely severed. You know it is still there when your baby whimpers softly in the night and that slight sound wakes you from a deep sleep, or when he sobs uncontrollably and you feel his distress as if it were your own physical pain.

You can attend prenatal classes, take a parenting course, read all the how-to books and magazine articles, and it will help. But nothing will truly prepare you for how completely different life will be during your first year as a mother. Your doctor can predict many of the physical changes you will experience postpartum, but you cannot anticipate how it will make you feel and how it will change your priorities and your goals—maybe even your politics.

There are many books available today that deal with the baby's first year, how he grows and develops, what he eats and when he sleeps. Each day is an evolution. Life for the new mother changes just as dramatically during those first twelve months. As the baby becomes the center of everyone's attention, a new mother must grapple not only with the basics of being an effective caretaker but also with the search for her new identity. She will never again be the same person.

This book explores the physical and emotional changes a woman experiences during her first year as a mother. It is a personal journey through my own first year, with stories from other first-time mothers who have shared their experiences and words of wisdom from various doctors, counselors, and other professionals.

I have taken a chronological approach, addressing each month of my baby's life as a separate chapter, but many of the subjects will overlap. While each month is dramatically different from the month before it, the topics remain much the same throughout the year. Feeding and diapering, for example—I was as concerned with what went into and what came out of my baby in the twelfth month as I was in the first month. The only difference was the nature of those substances both going in and coming out. During the year, we graduated from breast milk only to pot roast and potatoes, and diapering became an increasingly more odorous and challenging adventure.

The first few chapters will cover the most obvious topics—breast-feeding, bonding, recovering your prepregnancy body, sex, and postpartum depression. The next few chapters will look at work, travel, baby-sitters, and how to juggle being a mother, wife, daughter, sister, employee, and friend to all the people who were part of your life before your baby came along.

The First 12 Months of Motherhood will also address birth control, discipline, handling advice from family and friends, self-discovery, and society's expectations of the modern mother. In the final chapter, I talk with several other mothers about how they have evolved personally through their first year of motherhood, how they felt about marking their child's first birthday, the temptation to compare developmental milestones and what they would do differently if given a chance to repeat the year.

I had always thought you had to be an expert to write a book, and I certainly didn't feel like an expert at the beginning of this undertaking. But I spent the year learning something new every day—from my baby and from friends, doctors, lactation classes, parenting workshops, and even from strangers I encountered in waiting rooms, elevators, and grocery-store checkout lines. By the end of the year, I felt like a pro at this job, ready and willing to dole out advice to the novices coming along behind me.

I was thirty-eight when our son, Jesse, was born, and I had been married for a little over fifteen years. My husband, Harold, is ten years older than I and has a daughter from his first marriage. In our early years, we chose not to have a child together because we were both very involved in our careers—he in manufacturing management and I as a newspaper reporter. Both were demanding professions that left little time for raising a family. He was transferred several times, and it seemed that we were always just getting settled in somewhere when it was time to move again.

It just never seemed the right moment to think about having a baby. Maybe later, I told myself. Not yet, Mom, we're going to the Caribbean this year, and next year there's that summer trip to Wyoming, I told my mother.

When our work schedules allowed, we loved to travel and entertain. There was a delicious freedom and spontaneity about being married without children. It is a lot like being single. You care about your mate, are conscious of his needs, but you are not responsible for him.

Many of our friends were also still childless, busy with their own rise up the corporate ladder, and as the years passed, we settled into a comfortable routine. When I discovered I was pregnant after such a long time, I was at first terrified that it would change our relationship, threaten the balance we had achieved. The fear was quickly overridden, however, by the absolute joy that there was a part of us growing inside me. The birth of our son did change our lifestyle—no more spur-of-the-moment trips—but it has made our relationship stronger and given us a bond as a family that we did not have as a couple.

Am I the average first-time mother? Was the year typical? Those are hard questions to answer, because today's image of the model mother is evolving so rapidly. Twenty years ago, she was young and had been married only a short time. She had boundless energy and unquenchable optimism. She may have worried less about her child because she had not yet lived long enough to comprehend the dangers that lurked around every corner.

"Younger mothers don't seem to be as preoccupied by their babies as the women I know who waited a long time to start a family. They don't worry about every little thing," said Kelli, who was in her late thirties when her son, Jordan, was born. "We wanted a baby, waited for him for such a long time. I never knew I could love so much, or worry so much."

Today's average first-time mother is probably a little older—in her late twenties or early thirties—and has established a career and achieved a certain order, a predictable pattern to her life. She is in for a rude awakening.

"I have always been very list oriented, and I always used to do all the things on my list," said Karen, a first-time mother who laughs at friends' advice to "'just let it go.' Easier said than done. I see this one friend who has a baby, keeps an immaculate house, and has all these craft projects going on. It makes me feel so incompetent."

Like Karen and many other mothers I have met during

the year, I was very organized and efficient before my son was born. Now, a year later, I feel I have done well if I am only a month behind schedule.

The first year of motherhood is both wonderful and terrible, exhilarating and exhausting. As new mothers, we are admonished to cherish and savor every moment, but it is sometimes humanly impossible to enjoy being awake at 2 A.M., having your best dress stained with baby spit-up, or struggling with an 8-month-old who is no longer willing to compliantly lie still while you change his dirty diaper.

Many women say they feel a tremendous aloneness in the early days of motherhood, as if their particular trials, tribulations and triumphs are unprecedented. In a sense, they *are* unique, because each mother and baby is an original model; but we all go through the same things, and we can learn from one another. This book is intended to reassure new mothers that they are not the lone carrier of the maternal torch. We are all in this together.

Month One

ON-THE-JOB TRAINING

In the months before I delivered our son, I was very busy getting ready for the baby—buying furniture, putting up wallpaper, watching videos—with the pragmatic drive of someone embarking on a new job. I subscribed to parenting magazines by the gross, bought virtually every baby book on the shelf, asked countless questions. I was prepared. No sweat. Motherhood would be a cinch.

But as my water broke, all that practicality, all those perfect plans for how to be a perfect mother raising a perfect child rushed from my head with equally fluid speed. It wasn't the fear of a painful or difficult delivery that had me worried, it had been an uncomplicated pregnancy, and I was scheduled for an epidural. (None of this "natural" stuff for me, there is absolutely nothing natural about something the size of a watermelon being squeezed out of something the size of an orange.)

My fear came from the sudden awareness that I had no idea what I was doing. How could I possibly be responsible for another human life, especially one so frail, so vulnerable, so dependent?

I had never fed or diapered a newborn or held one for more than a few minutes. My experience with older babies was almost as limited, and the prospect of bathing my child, changing a diaper, or taking his temperature was frightening, to say the least. And breast-feeding? I just hoped he knew what to do.

I suddenly forgot everything I had read to prepare myself and began desperately to wish I had attended prenatal classes and paid more attention to my friends who had become mothers years before. I had enjoyed a successful career as a writer, lived in assorted parts of the country, and visited foreign lands. I was not an ingenue, yet I had absolutely no idea what I was going to do with this child once I got him home from the hospital.

Most hospitals offer classes in basic baby care, and you can always ask your pediatrician about those tasks you are uncertain of, but there will be many situations in those first few weeks you just can't anticipate.

It would be nice if you could rehearse a few things, but who are you going to get to volunteer for practice with a rectal thermometer? Sucking mucus out of a stuffed up nose and changing a boy's diaper without getting sprayed in the face are other skills the new mother can only learn through on-the-job training.

A few good books on basic baby care and health will be a big help. Look for a month-by-month guide with good illustrations—color photographs that show the difference between heat rash and chicken pox can be very useful.

Don't even try to read the entire book. You won't have

the time after the baby is born, and you probably won't remember much if you try to read it ahead of time.

New mothers unanimously agree that the ability to remember things (our name, for instance) suffers during those first few months of motherhood. Fatigue, often bordering on exhaustion, and sleep deprivation can make even the simplest task seem complex. In that first week at home, I found I could remember very little of the instructions the nurses gave me at the hospital on such matters as caring for the umbilical cord and the circumcised penis.

So many things will seem alien to you in the first few weeks. My pediatrician had cautioned me to keep track of how much the baby was urinating by counting wet diapers. I was using disposable diapers, and they were so absorbent that I couldn't tell whether they were wet or not. I'd put a finger inside the diaper and squeeze. Couldn't tell, so I'd try two fingers. Once, I accidentally squeezed him and was rewarded with a resounding cry of indignation.

At first I changed them every two hours, no matter what. I wonder how many diapers I wasted with that practice? I'm more than a little embarrassed to admit that I called my pediatrician to ask how to tell if a diaper was wet! She must have heard this question before, because she immediately suggested I place a folded tissue into the front of the diaper. This was a good indicator for wetness, but the sodden tissue would adhere to his penis, and by the time I would get all the little pieces unstuck, he had usually wet again, sometimes in my face, sometimes in his, sometimes out the window above his changing table. I guess aim is something that has to be perfected over time. I decided to let his father work on that one.

For a time, keeping an exact record of when he nursed and when a diaper was changed became an obsession. But I was so exhausted I couldn't keep track. I would fall asleep while breast-feeding him during the night and wake up wondering if he had just begun or just finished, or how many times he may have nursed while I slept. It was sort of like an all-night buffet that he could just keep coming back to for seconds or thirds.

At one point, during a moment of semi-incoherence, I considered taking a crayon and marking the wall beside our "nursing" chair. Several times I found myself digging diapers out of the wastebasket to count them at the end of the day.

Counting diapers was important in those early weeks. Our pediatrician said that is the best way to determine if a newborn is getting enough to drink and not dehydrating and if his kidneys and urinary system are functioning properly. But it didn't require the exactitude of scientific research. As long as he was wetting at least six times a day, there was nothing to worry about, she said.

Eventually, I realized that the need to monitor his diapers so closely was mostly for my benefit—to reassure myself that I was doing something right. Perhaps it made me feel more confident, more in charge, as if I knew what I was doing.

Months later, when I could spot a wet diaper at ten paces, I was able to laugh at that memory of how frantic I had been over this diapering dilemma.

The ability to laugh and a good baby book or two are necessities for getting through the first year. Gather all the information you can to help you emerge triumphant, but accept that you will make mistakes. Try to look at each misfire as an opportunity to learn.

It will be a long year, filled with joys, fraught with mishaps, overrun with conflicting emotions. You will experience frustration, anger, and, above all, love for the child to whom you are forever bound.

THE TIES THAT BIND

We mothers have been told—or perhaps we are telling each other—that we must bond with our baby the very instant he is born, if not before.

Anne, pregnant at the same time I was, talked to her unborn daughter, patted and cuddled her distended belly. Her devotion was obvious. I never really felt that link to the child growing inside me. I was emotionally detached during pregnancy and worried that I would never have that all-powerful maternal bond.

Despite the rush of emotion I felt when he was delivered and the desire to love and protect him, I still didn't feel that immediate connection. It didn't seem real as I watched the nurses clean him off and bundle him up in a blanket and cap that made him look rather like the title character in Dr. Seuss's *The Cat in the Hat.*

Except for being a little lighter on my feet, I didn't feel any different. I didn't feel like a mother. It was only after everyone had gone home and I was finally alone with my new son that I began to sense that maternal connection. I spent most of the night standing over his crib as he slept, marveling over his tiny hands and feet, wondering what he would be like.

Later, when I talked to other mothers during a lactation workshop, I discovered that my experience was not unusual. Those first feelings after delivery, they agreed, were not necessarily intense love and devotion. "I was just relieved that the labor was over and happy to have a flat stomach again," said Patty, as she nursed her 3-week-old daughter. "But now I just love her so much."

Many mothers experience a sense of detachment during pregnancy, as well as concern about what kind of mother they will be.

Many things about mothering are instinctive, but the kind of love that bonds you to another human being for the rest of your life takes time and nurturing to grow and develop. When it happens, you will know a love more profound than anything you have ever experienced before.

"I didn't know I could love something so much," Chalene said about her 6-month-old son, Skyler. We were at a social gathering, away from our children for a rare moment, and yet, like magnets, we were drawn to one another, eager to discuss our experiences as new mothers.

Before I joined this club, I loved to go to parties and move from group to group, joining in discussions of world events, politics, local gossip. Now I find myself gravitating toward the circle of mothers of young children. First-time mothers love to talk with other mothers, sharing ideas, comparing events, and asking questions that only another new mother would understand.

There had been several tragedies involving children reported on the news in the days preceding this party. We expressed sympathy for the families who had lost their babies. As new mothers, we could no longer be neutral in the face of such events. Each one seemed to touch us personally, to leave an ache in our hearts.

As Chalene spoke about the intensity of her own feelings, several mothers nodded their heads in silent agreement. Yes, we all loved our husbands dearly, and it would be tragic if something were to happen to them. But we could go on. The death of a child, however, would be devastating.

CRY ME A RIVER

One of the advantages of this intense love is an astonishing, almost miraculous improvement in hearing, especially when it comes to the sound of your own baby's cry. I've always had fairly good hearing, nothing remarkable, but now I can hear the slightest whimper from my son even when he is in his crib and I am downstairs amid the rattle of pots and pans and the blaring of the television. I marveled at this newly acquired "mother's ear." Not only could I hear his breathing change cadence, but I could also distinguish my baby's cry from the wail of other babies.

Jesse was born shortly before Christmas, and we had lots of holiday visitors. One afternoon the house was filled with family, including several young nieces and nephews. I noticed that when a baby cried somewhere in the house (they had been put down for naps in every conceivable corner), all the mothers instantly looked up with the same expression: head cocked to one side, eyes slightly glazed. It would be only a second or two before they would say, "That's not mine," and go back to their plate, or "That's for me," and be up and out of the room in a flash.

In a few short weeks, I was able to identify the different types of crying. Jesse's hunger cry would usually begin with a short burst, followed by a pause to catch his breath (and perhaps to listen for my approach). His angry cry was pitched lower and vibrated, while a cry of pain was high and shrill. His bored cry, a whiny sound, sometimes became his tired cry, a wail often accompanied by kicking feet, flailing arms, and a scrunched-up little red face that resembled one of those doll heads made from a dried apple. Thankfully, this cry lasted only a few minutes before he succumbed to sleep.

Coping with a crying baby was one of my greatest challenges as a new mother. I felt helpless, inadequate, and guilty—as if I were totally responsible for his tears. But the more I learned about why he cried and when he cried, the better able I was to calm him and to deal with my own emotions.

It helped to realize that not every cry meant he was suffering. Sometimes he just wanted attention or was sleepy. Every baby has his or her own pattern of crying, and each new mother, in time, finds what best soothes her child. For some, rocking or taking the baby for a walk in the stroller works, and most moms agree that a ride in the car almost never fails. Later in this book, you'll meet Jennifer, a new mom who spent three months driving around a parking lot near her home.

The hardest thing for most new mothers to accept is that sometimes babies cry for no apparent reason. You can attend to their basic needs, cuddle them, and comfort them, and still they wail incessantly. It may be tension, fatigue, or overstimulation. Maybe they just like the sound of their own voice. Sometimes you just have to wait it out. The good news is that newborns seem to cry a little less each day, and in time they become "settled" babies who cry much less often and are more easily comforted.

MOTHER'S TURN FOR TEARS

Dealing with your baby's heartrending sobs may be doubly difficult when you feel like dissolving into tears yourself. Estimates vary, but some doctors say 50 percent of women admit to experiencing some degree of depression following delivery. Others put the figure as high as 90 percent.

"I could just look in the mirror and burst into tears," my neighbor Shelley recalled when asked about her first week home with her new baby girl. There was no specific reason, she said, but it was about the time her milk "came in."

Fluctuating hormones are thought to be the primary culprit, but many other factors can contribute to the baby blues. Like many first-time mothers, I was overwhelmed by the responsibility and amount of work involved in caring for a newborn.

I felt uncertain, frustrated, and anxious. According to Depression After Delivery, a national nonprofit organization offering support to new mothers, this is a very common reaction, occurring in the first few days after delivery. I sent for D.A.D.'s brochure and packet of information on postpartum depression and was reassured to learn that I was not losing my mind and that I was not alone.

Hippocrates is thought to be the first physician to write about postpartum depression, some two thousand years ago, according to Dr. Susan Hickman, a noted psychotherapist who operates the Postpartum Disorders Clinic in San Diego. The clinic, which treats roughly a thousand patients a year, is one of only a few in the United States to focus exclusively on postpartum disorders. A similar clinic is operating on the East Coast in conjunction with a Boston-area hospital.

The baby blues aren't inevitable. It doesn't happen to everyone, but it is common. Approximately 80 percent of all new mothers experience unwarranted weeping, irritability, restlessness, impatience, and anxiety during the first few days after delivery, according to D.A.D. For most women, these symptoms are mild and disappear on their own within a few days or weeks. About 10 percent of all new mothers, however, will suffer a more severe case of postpartum depression.

The onset of PPD can occur anytime during the first twelve months postpartum, or even later if weaning is postponed past the first year.

"Most instances occur during the first two weeks. Cases which manifest later are usually connected with weaning the baby or the resumption of the menstrual cycle," explained Dr. Hickman, who has been treating postpartum patients for fifteen years.

Along with crying, women with PPD may also experience feelings of helplessness, anger, paranoia, compulsive behavior, over-concern for the baby, or a lack of concern for the baby. Professional treatment is usually required.

An even smaller proportion of women, one out of every thousand, experience severe postpartum psychosis, with symptoms often including delusions, hallucinations, suicidal thoughts, or attempts to harm the baby. Severe cases usually require extensive treatment, including medication, for several years.

Sleep deprivation does not cause postpartum depression, but it can exacerbate the problem.

"If a mother can't sleep, it's very important that she get treatment. If she can't get it from her OB, then she should seek help elsewhere," said Dr. Hickman. "Some women with early symptoms, if they are not nursing, can simply take a sleeping pill, get some much-needed rest, and be fine."

Most of the new mothers I shared with during my first year experienced minor baby blues that were quickly forgotten. The length and severity of the depression seemed to correlate with the difficulty of their birth and the existence of problems during the early days—breast-feeding difficulties, for instance, or health concerns, such as the jaundice so common during the first week.

I feel lucky not to have experienced a serious or prolonged bout of the baby blues, but I would not want to relive those first two weeks. Even though I doubted my ability to handle my new role as a mother, I also felt I couldn't trust anyone else (even my own mother) to watch him for me. To the point of paranoia, I imagined all sorts of catastrophes occurring in my absence.

I cried almost daily during those first weeks. Exhaustion and sleep deprivation had to have played a major role in this weepy phase. One afternoon I was selecting a baby photograph to send along with announcements when my mother commented that his eyes were shut in all of them and that made her think of the stillborn babies she delivered before my brother and I were born. I became virtually hysterical and cried for hours.

It took a few weeks (probably the time required for my hormones to reach some normal balance), but my daily bouts of crying did stop, and I was eventually able to leave my baby for an hour or two without having a panic attack.

Whatever degree of depression you sink into, having a supportive spouse will help, especially if he has a good sense of humor.

My husband came home one afternoon during that first week to find the whole house in tears. Mommy was crying, grandma was crying, the baby was crying, and the dog (a ninety-five-pound Doberman) was hiding under the coffee table. The baby had refused to suckle from my engorged nipples, and I had convinced myself that he would starve to death.

"Is this the postpartum depression you warned me about?" Harold asked as he took me in his arms and began to rock me as if I were the baby. After he had comforted me, he calmed the baby, let the dog out, and totally ignored his mother-in-law. Then he got out the breast pump I had forgotten (purchased way back when my brain was still functioning normally), read the operating instructions, and helped me pump enough milk into a bottle to fill our son's tummy and lessen the engorgement of my breasts. Later he proudly proclaimed that he could now boast of having milked holsteins, jerseys, and blonds.

Along with hormonal changes, exhaustion and sleep deprivation are also thought to contribute to depression following delivery. Sleep became a luxury, with feeding times coming every two to three hours, round the clock. I almost felt guilty that I enjoyed his naps so much.

All of these sensations combine to create an overwhelmingly intense period when your emotions will shift from ecstatic joy to great sadness with only the slightest nudge. This is a time of dramatic transition during which you will metamorphose from the woman you were into the mother you are to become. Enjoy the moment, savor the exhilaration, relish even the tears, for you will never experience this intensity of new emotions in quite the same way again.

If it becomes too overwhelming to handle, emotionally or physically, don't be ashamed or embarrassed to ask for help. It takes wisdom to recognize when you need help and courage to seek it before you reach the end of your rope.

LIFE ON THE MILKY WAY

Feeding your baby will consume most of your waking moments by the beginning of the second month. Whether you are breast-feeding or bottle-feeding, getting nourishment into your little one will be your priority.

Kimberly had come to visit when her newborn, Cassie, was just a little over a month old. Late the first night, I observed her in the kitchen, washing bottles to be used the next day, then preparing a couple to get her through the rest of the night. First thing the next morning, she was going through the same ritual—washing the bottles used during the night and filling fresh ones for the day. And at the end of the day, it was time to start all over again. A seemingly endless cycle.

Watching this, I was glad I had decided to breast-feed my baby—and had stuck to the decision despite those first almost unbearably difficult weeks. I only had to undo a few buttons and settle my son comfortably in my arms—no washing bottles and mixing formula at all hours of the day and night. I came to think of my breasts as nature's own MREs (the military's "meals ready to eat").

There are many advantages to bottle-feeding. There is no nipple pain or breast discomfort; the mother has more freedom and fewer demands. Because formula is harder to digest than breast milk, it seems to keep newborn babies satisfied for much longer periods of time, requiring a feeding every four hours instead of every two. There are no restrictions on the bottle-feeding mother's diet or choice of birth control, and (maybe this is the greatest benefit) someone else can get up for that 4 A.M. feeding.

Breast milk, on the other hand, is easier for the baby's under-developed system to digest, and allergies, constipation, and diarrhea are rarely problems for breast-fed babies. Many of the mothers I have met in recent months who chose to bottle-feed their babies had to switch from a cow's milk–based formula to a soy formula because of allergies or digestive problems.

My pediatrician and my obstetrician both extolled the blessings of breast-feeding. Even the manufacturers of infant formula agree that breast milk is best.

The maternity nurses at the hospital where I delivered also encouraged me to breast-feed. It means better health for the baby and less risk of diaper rash, and (this may have been the one that tipped the scales) they said I would lose weight faster.

I'm not sure that this promise of quicker weight loss was exactly accurate. True, lactation does help speed the shrinking of your uterus back to its prepregnancy size. And if you are nursing, you'll burn an extra 500 or so calories a day. What they don't tell you is that your appetite will increase while you are breast-feeding and you will probably consume at least that many extra calories to satisfy your hunger.

I was only a few months pregnant when I visited Jennifer and her newborn son, Collin. After nursing the baby, she rummaged around in the kitchen and came back with a plate of no-fat cookies.

"I'm always starved right after I nurse," she explained. "Actually, I'm hungry almost all the time."

My primary objection to breast-feeding had been its inherent restrictiveness. How could I schedule a life around this perpetual dinner bell? Would I become housebound by the embarrassment and dishabille of breast-feeding in public? Would my husband find it distasteful or be jealous of the intimacy it created between me and my child, something he could not share? Would I leak?

These were questions no one else could really answer for me. I talked with many experienced mothers during the last months of my pregnancy, searching for those answers. What I found was a wide range of opinions and attitudes. Some mothers breast-fed out of a sense of duty and were glad to wean at three months. Others couldn't tolerate it and didn't try or only kept at it for a couple of weeks. Still others found it exhilarating and were passionate in their extolling of its virtues.

I weighed all the advantages and disadvantages before I reluctantly made the choice to breast-feed. I knew it was the best thing for my baby, but I didn't know if it would be the best thing for me. I was not very enthused about the prospect.

I set a one-month goal and promised myself that if it wasn't too bad, I'd try for two. As the weeks and months slipped by so easily and so quickly, all of my earlier reservations disappeared.

Breast-feeding is restrictive, but I found that this doesn't bother me as much as I thought it would. While I am not as mobile as I was before I became a mother, I am perhaps less hampered than the mother who can't take the baby out without taking the time to prepare formula, bottles, and nipples to go. No matter where I'm going, or how long I'll be gone, I've got an ample supply of food for my baby. And it's free!

Leaking was another concern. Friends and relatives had complained about months of wearing soggy undergarments. Jennifer's first shopping excursion after her son was born ended in embarrassment when she heard someone else's baby crying.

"It was like a dam had burst—right there in the middle of Nordstrom's," she recalled.

The sound of your baby's cry—sometimes any baby's cry—causes a powerful hormonal reflex in a breast-feeding mother. Even thinking about a baby's cry can cause the nerves in the breast to signal the pituitary gland at the base of the brain to release oxytocin, the hormone that speeds through the bloodstream down to the tiny milk storage sacs in the breasts. The tissues surrounding these sacs tighten and force the milk down the ducts leading to the nipple. It sounds like a complicated, time-consuming procedure, but it happens in a matter of seconds. Just like turning on a faucet.

Not all women experience leaking while breast-feeding, the lactation specialist at the hospital told me. I bought a supply of breast pads just in case, but ended up giving them to my sister-in-law, who gave birth a few months after I did. The only time I experienced any leaking was on a trip to Alabama during the summer, when the humidity level surpassed the 90-degree weather.

Sweet Rewards

If you have made the decision to breast-feed for the first year, you have done yourself and your baby a great favor. It is one of the most rewarding and enriching experiences of motherhood. There is nothing comparable to that sensation of pure love flowing directly from your body into your infant. It is a sweet memory that you will carry with you for the rest of your life.

As natural as breast-feeding is, it is not necessarily instinctive. You will have a lot to learn, not only in the first few weeks but throughout the year as your baby's needs, and your own, constantly change. One of the best sources of information about breast-feeding I've found is *The Breastfeeding Sourcebook* by M. Sara Rosenthal. I will make several references to the book in the following paragraphs, in which I discuss some of the issues critical to successful breast-feeding during my own first year.

Getting started. The first week of breast-feeding is the most difficult, and it is during this time that many women give up because they lack the necessary knowledge, guidance, and support. Ask your doctor or hospital to refer you to a lactation specialist to help you through the first few weeks. She can help you find the most comfortable and efficient position for breast-feeding and will show you how to make sure your baby has latched onto the nipple and is suckling properly. She can also answer your many questions and ease your fears. If it had not been for my own lactation consultant, I would have given up during the first week because I was certain my baby would starve before my milk finally came in.

Jaundice. This is one of the most common excuses for abandoning breast-feeding during the first week. According to *The Breastfeeding Sourcebook,* roughly 50 percent of all normal, full-term infants have neonatal jaundice during their first week of life. Ninety-five percent of these cases involve normal, physiological jaundice in which the baby's skin turns yellow because red blood cells are producing more bilirubin than the baby's immature liver can process. This usually develops around the second or third day, peaks between the fifth and seventh days, and then begins to recede. Many women mistakenly assume it is their milk that is causing the problem and will stop breast-feeding when in fact this is one of the best treatments for normal jaundice. Bilirubin passes through the baby's stools, and the more the baby nurses, the more he poops, hence the faster bilirubin is eliminated. Even when breast milk is the culprit, it is rarely recommended that the mother stop breast-feeding. Breast-milk jaundice, which is believed to be triggered by some factor in the milk itself, only occurs in 2 to 4 percent of all neonatal jaundice cases, according to *The Breastfeeding Sourcebook.* Even without treatment, breast-milk jaundice usually clears itself up, although it may take a little longer.

What goes down will come back up. For the first six months, at least, spitting up will demand a lot of your attention. Rarely will you be able to wear an outfit without its being christened by your baby at least once, and probably more often. A cloth diaper draped across your shoulder will become an integral part of your wardrobe. The most common reasons for a breast-fed baby to spit up, according to *The Breastfeeding Sourcebook,* are too strong a letdown (in which case the baby will gulp too hard) and the baby's strong gag reflexes. (Spitting up is as common in formula-fed infants.) Babies may continue to spit up throughout the year, but the problem diminishes considerably during the second six months. In the meantime, keep the baby upright as much as possible and avoid bouncing him around too much after a feeding. (You might also advise your husband not to hold the baby up over his head until dinner has had time to settle sufficiently.)

Are you what you eat? I was constantly admonished about what to eat and drink and what to avoid while breast-feeding my baby. There are many dietary purists who believe you should eliminate all caffeine, chocolate, spicy foods, and anything that causes gas. It was once thought that a mother's diet greatly affected not only her ability to breast-feed but also the quality of her breast milk. More recent studies, however, have shown that even the poorest diets do not affect breast milk whatsoever and only mothers who are chronically and severely malnourished have reduced milk supplies. According to *The Breastfeeding Sourcebook,* some foods—chocolate, sugar, caffeine, garlic, onions, and cabbage, to name a few—can negatively affect your baby's digestive system. It's best to test these items one at a time, and if they don't appear to bother your baby, there is no need to cut them out of your diet. The primary reason why you should eat a healthy, well-balanced diet while breast-feeding is so you will feel better and have the energy to keep up with your little one.

Weight loss. One of the many myths surrounding breast-feeding is that nursing mothers will lose their pregnancy weight faster than nonnursing mothers. The truth is, some nursing mothers do seem to lose more weight, while others don't lose any extra weight at all. For some women, weight comes off more easily at the end of breast-feeding or even after weaning. Another myth is that a nursing mother needs to eat roughly 500 extra calories a day per baby above her prepregnancy calorie intake. This may be true for some mothers but not for all. Most lactation specialists advise nursing mothers to eat when they are hungry and stick to good foods, rather than junk.

Drink up. The need to down eight glasses of water a day is another myth often told to nursing mothers. Studies have shown that all this fluid does not improve, increase, or maintain milk production. Nutritionists will tell you to drink enough fluids to prevent dehydration and constipation. According to *The Breastfeeding Sourcebook,* you are probably getting enough water if your urine is pale yellow, rather than a darker shade. Along with water, other sources of fluid include fresh fruits, vegetables, soups, juices, and milk. Yet another old wives' tale is that a nursing mother must drink lots of milk. While this might be good for your own health, especially if you aren't getting enough calcium from other sources, how much cow's milk you drink has no effect on your production of breast milk.

Express yourself. There are so many factors involved in breast-feeding that no two women's experience will be exactly alike. Some women may need to express breast milk several times a day, while others may use a breast pump only a few times during the year. The mothers most likely to need to express breast milk are those who have gone back to work, but there are many other situations requiring a woman to pump her milk. If she is nursing more than one baby at a time and needs to build up her supply, pumping will encourage her body to make more milk.

If a mother has too much breast milk, pumping will prevent the discomfort of engorgement. If she must be separated from her baby or cannot nurse because she is sick or taking medication, pumping will keep the milk supply up until breast-feeding can be resumed. Pumping may also be necessary during weaning to relieve discomfort until your body has adjusted to a reduced nursing schedule. Expressing your milk is also part of the treatment generally recommended if you have a bout with mastitis.

Expressing your milk can become as easy and natural as breast-feeding if you have the right equipment and follow instructions carefully. It is important to find a good breast pump and become acquainted with its operation before delivery. There are several types of pumps available, or you can try your hand at manual expression. *The Breastfeeding Sourcebook* recommends an electric pump with an automatic cycle for the suction pressure. Avoid pumps that require you to turn the suction on and off yourself by sliding a thumb or finger on and off a hole in the suction system. I purchased this type of pump and was never very successful in pumping more than an ounce or two at a time. The larger, automatic cycling electric pumps are expensive, and it may be more economical to rent them from a hospital or medical supply company. It might also be wise to purchase a small manual pump to take when you are traveling and hauling around the larger electric model would be impractical.

Weaning. This is a fairly simple process, especially when compared to the first few weeks of breast-feeding. Whether you decide to wean at six months, at the end of the year, at eighteen months, or even later, the key word is *gradual.* Sudden weaning can be stressful for both you and your baby. Most babies take the lead in reducing the number of times they nurse as they consume more solid foods and other liquids and are generally down to four or five times a day by the ninth or tenth month. If you decide to wean at the end of the year, you can begin eliminating one nursing at a time around the ninth month. Every few weeks, simply replace a nursing with a meal or a snack. Don't feel guilty if you backslide from time to time. A sick, teething, or overtired baby may need an extra suckling. Traveling can also upset weaning schedules, but you can quickly get the process back on track once you are home and have restored your routine. The bedtime feeding, often the most precious for both mother and baby, is usually the last to go, although this will vary depending on your own situation.

Social pressure. The American Academy of Pediatrics recommends breast-feeding for a full year, and the World Health Organization suggests mothers breast-feed for two years, yet in America there remain many prejudices against breast-feeding, especially beyond the first twelve months. Despite my efforts to be very discreet when breast-feeding outside the home, I encountered some disapproving stares and comments during the year. Once, on an airplane flight, I nursed during takeoffs and landings and was told by the woman seated next to me that it made her uncomfortable. She said she was "not used to seeing that done in public." Even your very best friends and loving relatives can be among the worst saboteurs of your breast-feeding endeavors. Many of them, especially if they had their children ten or twenty years ago, followed the trend of their day and bottle-fed. It may be a touch of guilt that makes them speculate that your baby is too thin or too fat because you breast-feed or that he will become spoiled if you do not wean him at the age they consider appropriate. When you choose to breast-feed, you must expect to deal with a little controversy, so it is wise to arm yourself with as much information as possible regarding the physical and emotional benefits of breast-feeding for you and your baby.

IF AT FIRST YOU DON'T SUCCEED

It took about six weeks to develop a good breast-feeding relationship with my baby. I wanted to quit dozens of times, but always convinced myself to try once more before reaching for the bottle.

The first week was agony, waiting for my milk to come in and wondering whether or not it ever would. The lactation specialist at the hospital told me to be patient. But how could I, when each day passed and my baby was getting only a little colostrum as nourishment?

"Four or five days is typical, but you shouldn't worry about how long it takes your milk to come in," lactation specialist Mary De Nicola cautioned. "Sometimes it depends on how hungry the baby is and how soon he empties all the colostrum out of your breasts. It's not an exact science."

On the fifth day, just as she had predicted, my milk finally arrived. It was an overnight delivery. I went to bed worrying about my "starving" baby, only to awake the next morning with a pair of double Ds. I had never in my wildest dreams imagined myself being so well endowed.

The milk was finally in, but my breasts were so large and so tight that Jesse's tiny mouth couldn't fit over the nipple. He seemed as startled as I was. If he could talk, he probably would have said, "Mom, I ordered the economy models, not the deluxe set."

A few tears, a hot shower, and a breast-pumping adventure later, and I was down to a more reasonable size and ready to swing into action, so to speak.

The next several weeks were spent developing technique. My body was making milk, but I had to learn the correct way to hold a baby to my breast and how to position my nipple into his mouth so that he could suck properly. To some extent, I even had to learn how to relax enough for the milk to "come down."

Even Jesse had lessons to learn. Like all babies, he was born with an instinctive sucking reflex, but it took several days for him to learn that sucking would deliver the food that would ease the discomfort of his hunger.

Our first attempts were totally uncoordinated and usually resulted in a backache for me and frustration for Jesse, who wasn't very patient with my time-consuming fumbling. We just couldn't seem to get comfortable.

Harold tried to help. I realized how important it was for a new father to participate. I didn't want to exclude him from the breast-feeding experience altogether, even if our joint effort did look a little ridiculous. Imagine a large man holding a tiny baby in the palm of his hand, much as he would grasp a football, but aiming it at a breast rather than a goalpost. This wasn't very comfortable for any of us, but it did give us a good laugh, and that was probably what we needed most right then. It's hard to cry when you are laughing.

Eventually, I learned to use a pillow to cradle Jesse into the right position, whether I was propped up in bed or in a soft chair. By the end of the second month, I could feed the baby while sitting at the dinner table, holding him with one arm and feeding myself with the other.

I was very precise about the length of time he nursed, to the point of keeping written records in the beginning. A few months later, I couldn't even remember why I kept track so diligently. He was nursing on demand, and he demanded about forty minutes every two hours. It would have been simpler to just record those fleeting moments when we weren't nursing.

Everything is so intense during those first couple of months. Because of the insecurity born of my inexperience with babies, I thought everything I did, or didn't do, was critical to his well-being. What I had to learn through trial and error was that a normal, healthy baby is not all that fragile and that I can make a few mistakes without stunting his growth or warping his psyche.

By the time Jesse was 2 months old, breast-feeding had become second nature for both of us. Once we had mastered the technique, I found it to be a very relaxing experience. So relaxing, in fact, that I often fell asleep during the nursing. That's why it's a good idea to position the baby securely each time you sit down (or lie down) to nurse.

A friend related this new-mother story to me: Exhausted from lack of sleep, the young mother had dozed off in a chair while nursing her baby. She awoke with a start, knowing instinctively that something was wrong. The baby was not in her lap and not in the cradle beside her. She leaped up in a panic, then realized that her feet were weighted down. The peacefully slumbering baby had apparently slid out of her arms, off her lap, and down her legs to cradle in the soft folds of her robe.

Many nights I would awaken to find Jesse sleeping peacefully in my arms, a drop of milk trickling from the corner of those cherub lips. I came to enjoy those late-night feedings, despite my longing for eight hours of uninterrupted sleep. It became a very intimate, peaceful time that belonged only to me and my child.

A peaceful setting is imperative for successful breast-feeding. The lactation nurse at the hospital explained what a complex physiological process it was, involving mind and body interaction. It takes only seconds from the time you put your baby to your breast for the sensitive nerve endings there to send a message to your brain, which then orders the pituitary gland to release the hormone oxytocin. This triggers the storage sacs in your breast to contract and force the milk down into your nipple.

It's a chain reaction, but unlike dominoes falling, the process can be interrupted if you are upset or distracted. Tension, anxiety, and discord can sabotage your best efforts, especially during the first couple of months. Even self-consciousness can impede the relay of messages that trigger the let-down reflex.

"Are you getting enough rest? Is there something going on in your life—other than being a brand-new mom—that is causing stress?" the lactation nurse asked during a breast-feeding workshop when several mothers expressed anxiety that they were not producing sufficient milk. "You have to relax. Put everything but you and your baby out of your mind."

If I was tense or upset, which was fairly often during the first couple of months, the best place for me to nurse was behind a closed, sometimes locked door, through which even the most well-meaning friend or relative could not intrude.

Our house was very full during those days. We had a steady stream of in-town and out-of-town guests. I've never been able to have a visitor without feeling the need to entertain, to play the gracious hostess. But there were times I had to leave friends and relatives to their own devices as I slipped away with the baby for a private suckling.

It was several months later before I really felt comfortable nursing in front of people, even close friends or relatives.

No Need to Panic

You will get a lot of advice—from medical professionals, family members, friends, and even strangers who seem to feel that you become public property not just when you are pregnant but also after the baby is born.

The best advice I can give is something I didn't learn until late in the first month: Don't panic. And don't let anyone else instill panic in you. You can end up doing more harm than good when concern over your baby's well-being overrides basic common sense.

In those first few days, I was obsessed with Jesse's lack of a bowel movement. He'd had them in the hospital, so what was wrong now? I just knew it meant something was terribly amiss and that it was all my fault.

I am a modern, professional career woman, a journalist. I have chased after lawmakers and followed the legal trials of lawbreakers. I am tough. But when my newborn was 5 days old and still not eating well or having bowel movements, I found myself sitting in bed at 2 A.M. with him in my lap, saying things like "Please give Mommy some baby poop. Mommy just loves baby poop, yes she does."

One of the worst decisions I made during this time was to give him a laxative. I had pestered the pediatrician with my concern to the point that she suggested this treatment. It was one of the worst experiences I have ever had—knowing I was intentionally doing something that hurt my child. When my panic finally subsided (after talking to another mother who had gone through the same thing), I realized that all the baby needed was a little more time for his digestive system to begin functioning properly.

His symptoms didn't quite fit the description of full-fledged, severe colic, but he obviously was experiencing some digestive distress. He would cry inconsolably during the evenings, alternately scrunching his legs up and then stretching them out in a frantic kick. The crying seemed totally unrelated to his basic needs—his diaper was fresh and his hunger appeased.

It always seemed to begin about the time Harold would get home from work. I tried changing our schedule, but nothing made a difference. Like clockwork, he would begin to cry about the same time every evening.

I began attending weekly breast-feeding workshops in hopes of finding a solution to these nightly bouts. The lactation specialists called it the "witching hour." Many babies, they explained, will experience persistent, unexplained crying during the early evening hours.

It may be that the hustle and bustle of that time of day (dinner being prepared, father coming home from work) overloads their immature nervous system. I must admit, I've felt that way myself about that time of day—exhausted, overwhelmed by responsibility, sleep deprived, and without a clue as to what to fix for dinner. A good cry just might have made me feel better.

It did not help that various relatives said it must be my diet and advised me to give up all fibrous foods, dairy products, anything with chocolate or caffeine, and everything prepared with any spice or seasoning. With all this well-meant but confusing advice whirling around in my head, I considered giving up food and just taking a vitamin.

Thankfully, our pediatrician was more levelheaded. She said I needed a well-balanced diet, including fiber, to keep my system functioning properly and producing milk. Almost everything was all right in moderation. If I found a particular food (such as pizza with the works or chocolate) that seemed to cause the baby discomfort, I was to avoid it until his digestive system was more fully developed. That seemed almost too logical, too good to be true. But she was right.

Jesse also had jaundice on our third day home, which flung me into a panic attack. I went on yet another guilt trip, telling myself I should have kept him in the sun more on his first day home, instead of listening to those who told me to "get him in out of the wind."

During that first week, I was on the telephone with the pediatrician at least once a day. Her nurse came to recognize my voice.

Dr. Sheila Ponzio laughed when I apologized for being such a pest. "It's common," she said. "A lot of first-time mothers call every day for the first week, sometimes for the first six weeks." After the first six weeks, she said, most babies start to smile, and this response helps mothers relax a little.

"That smile gives them confidence, and by the second or third month, they feel like pros," Dr. Ponzio said.

She said the first-timers who tend not to call often are

those with mothers and grandmothers who live nearby. "It depends on what kind of support you've got, who you can turn to with experience, whether it is a relative or maybe a neighbor who has several children."

But no matter what kind of support she's got, it is important for a new mother to establish a good relationship with her baby's pediatrician during the first year.

"I like to feel that I am an educator, a facilitator. The old-style pediatrician was the authority, a father figure—a 'Don't make a move without asking me' type of physician," she continued. "I want parents to develop the confidence to handle most situations on their own. The relationship should be one of support."

I don't remember if my sense of confidence arrived with Jesse's first smiles, but it does seem that I stopped obsessing at about six weeks. I did continue to call our pediatrician at least once every couple of months, whenever I had a question about food, nursing, over-the-counter medications, or travel.

Life became a little easier when I accepted that when Jesse was hungry or sleepy or needed a diaper change, he would let me know, whether or not it fit into whatever schedule the pediatrician or those thousand and one baby books recommended. There really is no technical manual for mothering. You have to learn to trust your instincts and let your baby's health and happiness be your guide.

Month two

REWARD OFFERED

Six weeks. That's the magic number you will have heard about. The bench mark after which your body is expected to be back to normal. So they say.

Ideally, you have lost all, or at least most, of your pregnancy weight, and your stitches, if you had an episiotomy or a cesarean delivery, have probably healed. You can have sex again. Your boss (if you are employed) will expect you back at work, and your husband will go back to his old routine, leaving you to perform most of the household chores—unless you have one of those marriages I've read about where husbands do dishes.

At six weeks, your obstetrician will look you over, pronounce you physically fit, pat you on the head, and send you out into the world. "Have any questions? That's fine. See you for your checkup next year." Even your conscience will get into the act and tell you to get rid of the cleaning service you hired just before delivery It is time to take off the training wheels and get down to this motherhood business.

When I went for my six-week postpartum checkup, I felt neither physically fit nor emotionally ready for the task ahead. I had dark circles under my eyes, and my body still ached and made creaking and popping noises when I walked. Although I had lost all but five to ten of those stubborn baby pounds, there was no way my hips would fit into my prepregnancy jeans. This was not my body. Who took my body, and when were they going to bring it back? I considered offering a reward for its safe return.

I marched into my obstetrician's office ready to demand some answers. (Hormone fluctuations may make you a little aggressive.)

"What about this 'six weeks' thing? Is there something wrong with me?" I asked my doctor.

"Six is the right number," she said. "But six months is more realistic."

Physically, your body will recover from the birth enough to resume normal activities in about six weeks. But, she said, it will probably be six months before your body looks or feels anything like it did before you became pregnant.

"At six months, I knew I had made it," said Dr. Susan Blase, an obstetrician–gynecologist and herself a first-time mother. "I really don't remember the first four months. But, after about six months, I began to think more clearly and it was easier to concentrate, even though I didn't sleep through the night until she was 11 months old."

For Dr. Blase, returning to work when her daughter was 7 weeks old was a relief. "My baby had colic—a totally different experience from what I had expected. The fatigue was unbelievable. There was no relief. The baby would never sleep. She was either crying or eating."

After the colic, Sarah developed a persistent ear infection, and they were taking her to the doctor every other week.

"I kept asking myself, What am I doing wrong?" her mother said.

She dreamed during those first couple of difficult months that something had happened to the baby, that suddenly Sarah just wasn't there. Dealing with the guilt over having those dreams was almost as difficult as the sleepless nights, she recalled.

Guilt, she said, is one of the most counterproductive emotions a mother has to deal with. Each time your child is sick or injured, you feel personally responsible and therefore guilty, even if there was nothing you could have done to prevent it.

"You talk yourself into guilt. It would be great if there was something you could take to just get rid of it. You just have to learn to live with it," she said.

Being an obstetrician, Dr. Blase said, she was prepared for the sleep deprivation, but combined with the strain of constant worry and the normal emotional letdown following birth, it was almost unbearable. She was always on edge.

"When I finally got the strength to go back to work, it was a relief," she said.

Jennifer didn't have much relief from the colic her son experienced during this first three months of life. A few weeks after Collin was born, Jennifer's husband was temporarily assigned to supervise a construction project for his company 2,000 miles away.

Jennifer, a first-time mother, was left to deal with a fretful baby on her own. "He cried every day. It would start about five or six in the evening and go on for hours. Sometimes he would only stop crying when we were in the car—and the car had to be moving. If I stopped for a red light, he would start to cry again," she said.

"I spent a lot of nights driving around in the parking lot at the theater. There was little traffic and no red lights," she added, then recalled the night she lost it during one of Collin's colicky crying bouts. "He had been crying for hours. I was sitting on the couch, holding him and trying to comfort him. The cat walked into the room, directly over to me, and started biting me on the ankle, as if to say, 'I've had enough; make it stop.' I just started to cry and couldn't stop."

Even babies who don't experience colic are going to cry, especially during the first few months. Most mothers say there is nothing much you can do but grin and bear it, and hang on to the knowledge that it gets better each day.

Sometime during the second month, babies typically begin to "settle" a bit and will not cry as often. This is when most mothers begin to emerge from that thick fog that has enveloped them since delivery.

Although my head did seem to clear somewhat about that time (I could at least tell you what day it was with some degree of accuracy), I was still plagued with fatigue. My baby was taking every ounce of energy I had, and then some. There were times I felt resentment, maybe not toward the baby personally but at motherhood in general. There never seemed to be any time for me as an individual. I was no longer a person, just a pacifier with legs, existing only to serve the constant demands of this tiny human being who hadn't really even smiled at me yet. Did he appreciate all my sacrifices, I wondered?

I had gone from center stage, the glowing pregnant mother-to-be, to backstage and had become the nameless caretaker of this adored new star of the show.

"Your self-image is different, and you are no longer the center of attention, like you were when you were pregnant,"

Dr. Blase explained when I complained of the lingering fatigue and feelings of resentment.

"There is a lot of emotional letdown after you have a baby," she continued. "There is the fatigue and the feeling that you are not in shape. Even if you lose the pregnancy weight quickly, you may not be able to fit into your old clothes for quite a while, if ever."

No matter how much weight a woman loses, she said, only exercise will bring about the return of a flatter abdomen. Even exercise may not return your body to its exact prepregnancy shape. To facilitate delivery, a woman's joints loosen during pregnancy. Many women note an increase in dress or shoe size, even if their weight returns to normal.

Technically, a pregnancy lasts for nine months, give or take a few days. But in reality, the first three months after delivery are almost as difficult physically and emotionally as the last three months of the pregnancy.

Many mothers and obstetricians refer to these months as the "fourth trimester." In the last months of your pregnancy, you couldn't sleep because you couldn't get comfortable; now you don't sleep because you are feeding and changing the baby every two hours.

You still don't have control of your bladder. You aren't going to the bathroom every twenty minutes, but when you do go, you aren't able to stop the flow at will, and you may leak some urine between times.

While I was pregnant, I came to terms with the realization that my body would probably never be quite the same again. I knew that there would be some vaginal stretching, that my hips might always be just a bit wider and that my hair might darken and change texture. I had been forewarned about these tribulations by other new moms.

What I didn't expect, two months after delivery, was to still feel as if something was about to fall out of my body. When I went in for my checkup, I discussed this sensation with my doctor. An examination revealed that it was a drooping bladder, pushed downward by the weight and position of the baby.

This bulge is commonly the result of weak muscle tone in the vaginal wall that supports the bladder, my doctor explained. The bladder pushes through this weakened musculature, causing a hernia. It may be small and virtually unnoticed, or large enough to be visible and uncomfortable.

"A woman often has some bladder changes after pregnancy. It may never go entirely back to normal, exactly as it was before," my obstetrician explained. "There could always be some discomfort if she had stitches or lacerations from a vaginal delivery. Even with a cesarean, there may be some vaginal laxity. It may always feel a little different."

I have talked with many mothers who experienced bladder problems following childbirth. The more children they had, the more severe the problem became, with some requiring surgery to tack up the bladder in order to stop leaking and prevent chronic infection.

Dr. Blase did not recommend surgery for my much less severe situation, but she did echo what I had already read in countless predelivery literature: Do those Kegel exercises. Do them while you nurse, she said, and when you're reading (as if I had time to read), watching television, or driving down the freeway. They are easy to do and unobtrusive. No one will know what you are doing, she said—unless you make a funny face.

This "perineal squeeze" is an isometric exercise you do by alternately contracting, then relaxing the area between the vagina and the anus. This is the same muscle that allows you to stop the flow during urination. Exercising it not only promotes healing by improving circulation in the area, Dr. Blase said, but it also will help you regain vaginal tone and push the bladder back into its prepregnancy position.

So, I went home to do my exercises, somewhat disappointed that the doctor didn't have a magic pill to pull my sagging parts together again and give me the energy to bounce through this fourth trimester.

I felt more than a little overwhelmed later as I nursed the baby on one breast, pumped the other breast, tried to read yet another book on basic baby care and did my Kegels to a four-beat rhythm: Pump, pump, squeeze, hold; pump, pump, squeeze, hold. All while trying to relax and enjoy it. Right. I wanted to scream. I wanted one of those bubble-bath, "take me away" moments. I wanted to be on a tropical island sipping something tall and frosty.

STEPPING OUT

If you are breast-feeding, you probably won't leave the house for more than an hour or two during the first month, and while you are away, you will just know your baby is in distress. Even if you are bottle-feeding your baby, you still probably won't get out much during those early weeks. If anxiety over your baby's well-being is going to prevent you from enjoying any of that free time, you may wonder, "Why bother?"

By the second month, however, you should begin to make the effort to leave the nest. Isolation is not healthy, and what is not healthy for you is not good for your baby. Going out to dinner or a movie, just you and your husband, or joining a group of friends for a girls' night out can do wonders to restore your spirit and make you forget that you are only getting a few hours of sleep each night.

Jesse was almost 2 months old when I joined a group of women for a game night. It felt great to dress up in something that didn't resemble maternity wear and to see a few fresh faces. Of course, I took along a photo album and called home at least once an hour.

Any opportunity to talk about your birth experience and to tell someone how wonderful your new baby is will invigorate you. For a little while, the spotlight will again be on you, as you regale friends with the story of your delivery and flash first photographs. You'll be in such good spirits by the time you get home that you'll hardly mind being up the rest of the night.

Sharing your feelings as a new mother is a wonderful antidote for those first-month baby blues. As your baby grows, becoming more independent and less fragile, you may not need the frequent support of other mothers, but during those early months, nothing will be as helpful or as reassuring as talking with other women who are feeling the same emotions and experiencing the same joys and sorrows.

Many cities have support groups available to new mothers. Check with local churches, mental-health departments, and the hospital where you delivered.

St. Jude's Medical Center in Fullerton, California, the hospital where I delivered Jesse, offers a weekly breast-feeding workshop for new mothers. Not only did it provide me with a wealth of information about breast-feeding, but it was a great opportunity to talk with other first-time mothers who were having the same difficulties that I was experiencing.

Most of the new moms attend only four or five classes during the early weeks, but they often come back when their baby is a few months old.

"Some even come back a year later, when they have new problems or concerns," said Ms. De Nicola, a lactation consultant with fifteen years' experience in coaching new mothers in the art of breast-feeding.

If it is mostly companionship you are looking for, check out a nearby chapter of the MOMS Club (Mothers Offering Moms Support). The MOMS Club is a national, nonprofit support group. The group has monthly meetings and weekly activities, including field trips, park days, play groups for children, speakers, community-service projects, and a baby-sitting cooperative. There are 200 chapters nationwide, but the organization is heavily concentrated in California, where the first club was established.

The group is open to both working and stay-at-home moms, but most of the programs are planned during the day and are therefore more convenient for at-home mothers.

"I had just had a baby and found myself at home with nowhere to go," said Terry Storm, president of the Yorba Linda MOMS Club. "Basically, I was lonely. I didn't know any other stay-at-home moms."

Terry said she never questioned her decision to stay home rather than return to her job. "I just didn't know how hard it was going to be on me emotionally. The MOMS Club gave me a reason to get out of the house. It helped keep me from being depressed."

I felt awkward and a bit shy when I attended that first MOMS Club outing—a breakfast at the local pancake house. I was fifteen minutes late getting there. A last-minute diaper explosion had required a quick bath and a change of clothes for both of us.

I never used to be late. Being on time was a priority for me, almost an obsession. Since becoming a mother, sometimes I'm running so late, I just don't go.

When I arrived at the MOMS Club breakfast, I apologized profusely for being late. The old-timers smiled. No problem; just got here ourselves, they said, as they juggled high chairs, strollers and car seats amid the cacophony of crying babies, whining toddlers, and clattering dinnerware. Two of the children, both about a year old, were doing a balancing act along the back of the booth while banging the window with their "sippy" cups. Juice was coming down like big, fat spring raindrops. I began to feel at home.

Here were twenty complete and total strangers, women I had never seen before. I didn't even know their names, yet I felt that common bond of motherhood. We were all in this together, sharing the joy, the trauma, and the challenge of raising another human being.

I was sorry that it had taken me so long to find such a support group. It wasn't a lack of availability. There are many organizations that offer such opportunities. City recreation departments may sponsor mother-and-baby exercise classes or group stroller walks, and some businesses, such as Gymboree, offer age-appropriate parent-and-child play programs. The Newcomers Clubs feature baby-sitting cooperatives and special activities for women with children. In the San Francisco area, there is Las Madres, a support group that matches mothers of children born in the same year.

Groups like these often offer something to do every day of the week, from park or mall stroller days and play groups to shopping excursions and mothers' nights out. Some areas have groups formed especially for mothers who have returned to the workplace. They share many of the same problems as stay-at-home moms, but they also face other challenges as well.

Along with some much-needed socializing, these groups can provide you with a place to sound out your fears and anxieties. Is my baby eating enough? Is he too fat, too skinny, developing motor skills when he should? I try not to make too many comparisons between my baby and other babies, but sometimes it helps to know what to expect. And you will get the most realistic answers from other mothers.

SEEKING SUPPORT

Most new moms feel isolated and alone in dealing with postpartum emotional and physical adjustments. The best thing you can do for yourself and your baby is to seek the support and companionship of other mothers. Here's a list of some of the organizations that offer help for new moms:

MOMS Club (Moms Offering Moms Support)
25371 Rye Canyon
Valencia, CA 91355

Depression After Delivery—National
P.O. Box 1282
Morrisville, PA 19067
(215) 295-3994 or 1-800-944-4773

La Leche League International
1400 North Meacham Road
Schaumburg, IL 60173-4840
(708) 519-7730

National Organization for Mothers of Twins Clubs
12404 Princess Jeanne NE
Albuquerque, NM 87112-4640
(505) 275-0955

No Room for Romance

There is very little time for anything but your baby during the first couple of months. Your husband may be bringing you flowers and candy and gazing after you like a puppy, tail wagging, drool puddling on the floor at your feet. Romance will be put on the back burner, or maybe even stored in the freezer compartment for a few months.

Despite hubby's obvious adoration (the likes of which you probably haven't seen since your honeymoon), sex will be one of the last things on your mind right now. At this point, the only thing most new mothers want to do in bed is sleep.

A lack of sexual interest is very common in the first few months following the birth of a baby. It doesn't happen to all women, and most of those who experience it say their libido returns (almost) to normal within a few months.

Your physical recovery—whether or not you are feeling pain—and your body's continuous hormonal fluctuations can greatly influence your sexual drive and your attitude toward your spouse.

Even some husbands will experience symptoms of a limping libido during these early months, especially if they are doing diaper duty and sharing in the sleepless nights. Instead of thinking about coital bliss and the new size of their wife's breasts, they may be laying awake at night contemplating life-insurance policies, the cost of braces, and college tuition.

Several women in my mother-baby play group complained that their husbands, instead of staying home where they were needed, worked overtime or took on second jobs during those early months. They probably weren't running away from their responsibility as a father but had succumbed to the panic caused by this newfound pecuniary obligation.

Pain, fatigue, stress, and the overwhelming responsibility of taking care of a baby will take their toll on even the most passionate romance. An extra hour of sleep can, at times, be much more appealing than an amorous interlude with your mate.

Each new mother I talked with described a slightly different experience. Many said they were just too tired to think about sex in those first couple of months, while others expressed a fear of getting pregnant again and complained of the loss of privacy with the baby still sleeping in their room, or, in some cases, in their bed.

Karen, married for six years before her son, Garrett, was born, said having a baby in the house did put some strain on her marriage, but overall has had a positive effect.

"This first year has been difficult in that our attention for one another has been divided by the baby's need for constant attention. Despite that, it has strengthened the bond between us," Karen said. "We are more comfortable with each other now. We are perfectly content staying home at night watching the baby play instead of going out."

Another concern frequently mentioned by new mothers is episiotomy discomfort, during or after intercourse. At six weeks postpartum, my obstetrician said, most women are safely past the danger of ripping out any stitches, but they may have some pain from the incision for several months to come. Even a year later, she said, many women experience tenderness in the episiotomy area.

A few lucky ladies do experience an increased sexual drive during those first few postdelivery months. The increased blood flow in the pelvic area can heighten erotic sensations, as can the breast sensitivity a woman feels during the first months of breast-feeding.

I was thankful to fall somewhere in that luckier category.

Despite lack of sleep and general exhaustion, I actually felt a greater sense of sexuality during those first couple of months. Breast-feeding, while not necessarily a sexual behavior, is certainly a sensual endeavor, and it made me feel more feminine, more womanly, and more desirable than I had felt in quite some time. Having a body that no longer looked like a late-season butternut squash (narrow at the stem and wide at the middle) was also something of an aphrodisiac.

Most doctors recommend you wait six weeks before resuming sexual relations, but that doesn't mean you can't express your love and affection in many other ways. I was very conscious of the need to touch my husband as much as possible during this waiting period. A brief caress on the cheek as I passed by on the way to the laundry with yet another armload of wet sheets and blankets, a foot fondle under the table during dinner, or a back scratch when we finally did manage to crawl into bed at the same time helped to keep the flame fanned.

Eventually, when your baby is older and begins to sleep at somewhat predictable times (some mothers say this doesn't happen until they start school, and then you can only predict that they will sleep late in the mornings), you can schedule those romantic interludes. You can try making a "date" or simply be prepared to drop everything and head for the bedroom as soon as the little darling goes down for his Sunday morning nap.

Month three

HELLO, MY NAME IS MOM

He laughed. That first joyful giggle, the result of a tickle to the tummy, brought me suddenly to the realization that Jesse was not just a tiny baby in need of my love and vigilant care. He was not a placid little lump of dough that I could mold into the child I wanted him to be. He was a developing person with a sense of humor and a very definite personality.

All of the baby experts say you should talk and sing to your newborn, but I felt awkward, as if I were talking to myself. Chatting to my baby with ease was something I had to practice at, a skill to develop over time.

I kept silent when others were around, and at first Jesse didn't seem to pay a great deal of attention to my running commentaries as I changed his diaper, bathed him or carried him around as I completed various household chores. By the time he was 3 months old, he seemed not only to be listening but to be enjoying the higher-pitched sound of my baby talk. The more he responded to my voice, the more comfortable I felt with our "conversation." By the end of the year, I didn't care who heard me chattering, or singing show tunes for that matter, as long as it kept him entertained while I finished my grocery shopping.

I knew that I probably would use baby talk—all parents do. But I did not expect to speak like the Queen Mother: "We are having our bath now. We are eating lunch. We are going to put our booties on so we can go to the store." Life had become a plural adventure. I was no longer a single entity.

At three months, he would smile at me whenever I walked into the room or bent to pick him up. Of course, he smiled at almost everyone at this point, but I liked to think his widest grins were reserved for me and his daddy. These first smiles and the sound of his laughter were all the reward I needed to compensate for the sleepless nights and demanding days. Most of the time.

This was an extraordinary stage of motherhood, when my baby and I were really getting to know one another. I was learning to think of him as an individual, and he was beginning to recognize me as his "special" person. There will be many special people in his life—grandparents, siblings, baby-sitters—but a baby's mother is almost always his first love.

It has been a few years, but I can still remember the sensations of first love. The feelings a new mother has for her baby are quite similar. You thrill with the newness of the emotion and you are touched by the sweetness, the tenderness, the innocence.

I wanted very much to be Jesse's first love, to see that look of absolute trust and adoration in his eyes. But I realized that this is not a genetic given. He will not love me just because I gave birth to him. I knew I had to earn that devotion with love. I didn't want to become so wrapped up in taking care of his physical needs that I neglected to give him the affection and playfulness he also needed from me.

I was often so consumed by the demands of mother-hood during those first few months that I forgot to take the time to enjoy all the special moments and to relax and simply play with my baby, or cuddle him even when he wasn't crying to be held.

I bought a journal before Jesse was born, so that I could record every moment. Unfortunately, I was too busy during the first two months to find a moment to record those moments.

At three months, Jesse and I were both more settled, and I was able to begin sneaking a little time for myself to write down my thoughts and feelings, to preserve each new expression on his face, every achievement.

LET'S PLAY BALL

Like most first-time mothers, I am constantly referring to the baby books. At first I read daily about basic baby care, illness, and feeding. By the third month, I was searching for the chapters on how to play with him, how to stimulate him, and how to chart his physical growth and social development.

Of course I worried that he would not develop as he should unless I did everything the experts suggested. We made numerous excursions to the toy store. He wasn't old enough to ask for anything, but I couldn't seem to resist all the brightly colored, noisy baby baubles. We bought teething rings and rattles, a telephone, his own pager and, of course, a television remote control. Like father, like son, the remote control was his favorite. He would cry whenever I tried to take it away from him—and so would the baby!

After the credit-card bill for my toy-store purchases came, I decided to look around the house for new items to satisfy his insatiable curiosity. I was surprised (and a little chagrined) to discover that wooden spoons, measuring cups from the kitchen and the cardboard cylinder from a roll of paper towels pleased him just as much as the expensive, battery-operated, some-assembly-required toys.

I also learned to give him some time to play by himself. I don't want to raise a child that must have constant companionship. I want him to know I am here if he needs me, but that he can enjoy spending time on his own, rattling his rattle, chewing the ears off his cuddle bunny, and sucking his own toes.

THE RHYTHM METHOD

"Oh, really?" my girlfriend said when I told her my baby didn't exactly have a schedule. Her tone of voice implied censure, as if I were remiss for not having more structure in my life.

We were trying to plan lunch, and she wanted to arrange to meet between feedings, diapers, and naps.

"No problem," I replied. "I'll just bring the baby along, and if he gets hungry, I'll just flop it out and feed him at the table."

"Oh, really?" she repeated. She said that a lot during lunch. She's unmarried, childless, and hasn't called me since. (More later on keeping and losing friends.)

I felt a little guilty that we had not established a routine by three months. Our life moved to a rather irregular rhythm. I knew Jesse would wake early, around 5:30 or 6 A.M., and nurse for almost an hour. Then he might nap for a while, maybe a half hour, maybe two hours. Or not. Then he would nurse again, play for a while, and maybe take another nap before nursing again. The rest of the afternoon would fall into a random pattern of nursing and napping.

Some days he would be down for numerous short naps, while other days he would sleep once or twice for three or four hours each time. I learned to be flexible. I also learned that as long as I kept his tummy full, I could drag him along on various outings no matter what the time of day. There were several occasions when I nursed him in a parked car between errands, or in the dressing room of a clothing store as my companions tried on clothes.

I could feed him, put on a fresh diaper, strap him into the car seat, and dash to the grocery store. Often, he would sleep while I wheeled up and down the grocery aisles. If I was quick, I could drive home and have the groceries put away before he awoke for his next feeding.

When I was working in a busy newspaper office, I lived by the clock. I always had daily "to do" lists, both for home and for work, and would methodically check each item off as it was completed. After the baby was born, I stopped even wearing a watch.

The only thing I was fairly consistent with was putting him to bed in his cradle at about the same time each evening. I realized that I would soon have to begin manipulating some semblance of a schedule into our day. But at this point, I was mostly just grateful that he had begun to sleep through the night.

SWEET DREAMS

Sleeping through the night. This joyous event began to occur around the end of the third month. The first night that he didn't wake me up around 2 A.M. to nurse, I was up at 2:01, hovering over his cradle, frantic that something was wrong. He was sleeping so peacefully, so quietly.

I actually missed the noisy sounds he made in his slumber as a newborn—the snorting and rattling that had me so worried at the time. One of the baby books described this as a "snurgle," and my pediatrician said it was nothing to worry about in a baby a few weeks old. It usually disappears by the third month.

But on this night, there was no snurgle. He was so silent, I couldn't tell if he was breathing. I wanted desperately to pick him up, but knew this would wake him and lead to a forty-minute nursing. I looked longingly at my bed but couldn't bring myself to leave the cradle without reassuring myself that he was alive.

I trained a tiny flashlight onto his face, but it was so still. I stole a drop of water from the glass beside my bed and placed it on his cheek to see if he would flinch. He didn't budge. I could feel panic bubbling to the surface, then I had another idea.

I slowly, stealthily stuck a finger into his mouth. He didn't wake, but his sucking reflexes were immediately alerted, and he began to pull at the intruding digit. After a moment, I slid my finger out gently and went back to bed.

I felt proud of myself. At least I had not attempted to crawl into the crib with him as did Shirley McLaine's character in the movie *Terms of Endearment.* I have watched that movie a half dozen times and always viewed the mother as a caricature, a gross exaggeration of maternal paranoia. Now I can relate. Been there, done that.

It was weeks (OK, maybe it was months) before I stopped checking on him throughout the night. I was able to wean myself down to only one or two peeks into his room during the twilight hours. Drinking a big glass of water right before you go to bed (a tip from my brother-in-law, Robert) will help to ensure you wake at least once during the night. You can slip into the nursery and tuck the covers back around your soundly sleeping child on your way back from the bathroom.

Once I had gotten past this phase of maternal neurosis, I was amazed at how a good night's sleep—several in a row, in fact—changed my view of the world. The sun seemed to shine a little brighter. Or maybe it was that I finally had the energy to go outside and look up.

RIDING OFF INTO THE SUNSET

Moving Jesse into his own room was another momentous, almost traumatic, episode in our first year. Not for the baby. I don't think he noticed. It was his mother who had trouble loosening the apron strings. I don't know why they call them apron strings. I don't wear an apron, and these strings led directly to my heart, not my waistline.

Before Jesse was born, I was reluctant to have him sleeping in our room, it would be disruptive to our sleep, infringe on our privacy, put a damper on our sexual activities, etc. This reluctance was yet another symptom of my struggle against succumbing to motherhood. I've heard many other mothers-to-be express similar concerns about giving up their freedom and independence.

But those first few weeks home from the hospital, I found I could barely even stand to put him in his cradle six feet away from me. I wanted him into the bed beside me, where I could feel him breathing. Eventually, I did move him into his cradle, realizing it meant a better night's sleep for all concerned, but for weeks I would drag the cradle as close to the bed as possible so I could stick my hand through the railing and touch him while he slept.

And now, the next hurdle. I guess these are the small first steps a child takes in leaving his mother's side. Today his own room, tomorrow he'll be wanting an apartment at the beach with the guys. It is a good thing mothers must let their children go a little bit at a time. If we didn't, the sight of our 18-year-old riding off into the sunset, surfboard strapped to the back of his red convertible, would undoubtedly kill us.

IN SICKNESS AND IN HEALTH

Every mother must pray that her child will never get sick, that he will be spared even the most common of colds, at least during that first, vulnerable year. It is natural to want to shelter your baby from illness and injury. Waking up to find him not breathing is an almost constant fear during the early months. I thought maybe I was being paranoid, but all of the mothers I have since met say they experienced the same ceaseless worry.

Mothers, new mothers in particular, can talk themselves into tremendous guilt and needless worry, my obstetrician said. "There is no way to avoid it; you just have to struggle through it. It's innate. Talk to your mother, your grandmother. They all went through the same thing," Dr. Blase said.

"And the worry never really goes away, not even after your children are grown," she continued. "My mom has told me that she still keeps her door open at night when we are home for a visit, just so she can hear if we need her during the night."

My own mother still waits up for me if I am out late during a visit home to Alabama. I'm 38 years old and still have a curfew.

Jesse's first illness, a common cold, was a minor one. Yet, I still worried that it was more serious than it seemed, that I wasn't diagnosing the symptoms right. I wanted to rush him to the doctor's office, but I settled for a telephone call instead.

Jesse started sniffling and sneezing a few days after a family get-together and, sure enough, at least one of the kids who had been there was sick the next day. I guess there is no way you can protect your child, short of total isolation for both of you, and that would be hazardous to your mental health.

I struggled through the next few days, coping with a fretful baby, anxious over his slight fever, and worried that I wasn't taking his temperature correctly and that I wasn't getting enough medication down his throat before he spit it back out at me. I asked our pediatrician if I would ever stop being so worried that I was not doing the right thing. Probably not, she said, especially with a first child. By the time you have a second or third child, you realize they are pretty tough and if you use a little common sense, you're probably not going to kill them.

As I was agonizing over my child's relatively minor ailment, I learned that a friend was dealing with a much more critical situation. Her 9-month-old son had pneumonia, immediately followed by roseola.

Roseola, her pediatrician told her, is an inexplicable high fever often accompanied by a rash all over the body. It sometimes follows a viral illness and is not considered a serious condition unless the fever becomes high enough to cause convulsions.

Chalene's son, Skyler, didn't have to be hospitalized, but they had to visit the doctor every day for weeks.

"I was just freaking out," Chalene said. "I was so worried I wondered if I was going crazy. I felt so bad for him, but there was nothing I could do. It was a helpless feeling."

Every time Skyler is sick, Chalene said, she feels guilty, as if his illness was her fault. She had to make several trips from her home in California to visit her family in Texas during Skyler's first year and agonized over exposing him to so many strangers.

"He's been flying since he was 2 months old, and every time we've gone somewhere, he's gotten sick with a cold, a runny nose, or an ear infection. The pediatrician said it was the change in cabin pressure and the recirculated air in the plane," she said.

Chalene said she had promised herself that she would be a "cool mom" who didn't panic and rush to the doctor with every minor ailment. "I'm not a worrywart. That's just never been my personality. But I worry now. I'm always reading my baby books, trying to diagnose things and treat him myself, but if he has a fever for more than three days, we're off to the doctor."

It was nice to know that somebody else spent as much time as I did reading baby books. There is no operating manual for a baby, no textbook to teach you how to be the best mother you can be, but gathering as much information as possible will help.

It's frightening when our children are sick, even when it is not a life-threatening illness, because it reminds us of how fragile they are, how tenuous is the miracle of their existence. I have yet to meet a mother who would not gladly take all of the pain, every bruise, scratch, cold, and flu that comes her child's way.

HELLO, MY NAME IS MOM 57

I'll Be There for You

I listened to the title song from the television series *Friends* and wondered how many of my friends would still be there for me in a year's time. Any major change in your life will affect your personal relationships, and motherhood represents a lifestyle shift of earthquake proportions. I needed my friends more than ever, but I didn't have the time or the energy to nurture these relationships.

Most of my premommyhood friends fall into either of two categories: The first group doesn't yet have children. They plan to—someday, maybe. Right now they are busy climbing the corporate ladder, establishing their own businesses. Motherhood will just have to wait. The second group married and had their babies when they were very young and now have teenagers too busy with school and friends to need or want much of their mother's time and attention. These moms are focusing on careers or have gone back to school.

Becoming a new mother has dramatically changed my relationship with both these groups, just as it has made a distinct difference in my association with acquaintances who do have small children at home. I was surprised to realize how few of my friends had small children. Unconsciously, I suppose, I cultivated friendships with women who shared my interests and lifestyle. I had little in common with mommies then, but once my existence became baby-centered, I wondered what common ground I would find with my old friends.

Finding myself on the other side of the play yard, I was drawn closer to women with babies and toddlers. But I didn't want to cast my old friendships aside. I had become a different person, and I was not sure these longtime relationships would survive the change.

On a trip home to Alabama, I visited a couple of old friends. They'll hate that phrase; perhaps I should change it to "friends I've known forever." Probably won't care much for that one, either.

Gayla was recently divorced, and her only child, a son, is now a college student. She often talks about him—his scholastic achievements, sports, and girlfriends. But she doesn't speak with the obsession of a new mother, and I knew I would soon bore her with talk of diapers and teething and feeding schedules.

We used to have so much to talk about on these visits home—men, parties, trips to exotic places, whose wives were sleeping with whose husbands, who'd had her tummy tucked and her breasts done and other titillating small-town gossip. I was determined not to monopolize the conversation with baby stories, but consequently found myself with very little to say. I couldn't seem to concentrate on any other subject for very long.

Motherhood, however, seems to have drawn me closer to Margaret, whose three daughters are now teenagers. She was excited for me and, I think, just a little bit envious. It would be nice to have a little baby around again, she said, but after watching a couple of diaper changes and a spit-up or two, she decided she could make do with borrowing mine for a little while.

Back home in California, Barbara, another sort-of-single friend (that means separated but dating her husband—hey, it's California), invited me to join her and a group of five or six other women on an outing to see an art exhibit and have dinner. Harold was out of town, I hadn't left the house in days, and I really felt the need to get out into the real world again. But I could not bring myself to leave Jesse with a sitter for so many hours. I used breast-feeding as an excuse, but in all honesty, I just couldn't bear to be without him for that long.

There are still times when I have to force myself to go out. I feel almost desperate for the company of other adults and for a chance just to get away from the house. Yet, at the same time, I find it hard to remove myself from my child. The separation is almost a physical pain, a dissection, as if a limb had been wrenched from my body.

So, when Barbara called, I bundled him up and gave him his first taste of culture—if you can call an exhibit of John Lennon's artwork culture. Had he been old enough to understand it, I probably would have covered his eyes.

At three months, it didn't bother me too much that I had become as dependent on my baby as he was on me. I knew that in time we would both begin to move ever so slightly apart, as he begins to explore the world on his own and as I begin to find a place in my new world.

Once you become a mother, you never go back to being exactly the same person you were before, even if you keep the same friends, return to the same career, and take up old hobbies and interests as your child grows and becomes less demanding of your time and energy. In the early months of motherhood it may seem hard to remember who you were before your baby was born. Vaguely you will recall being a wife, friend, employee, volunteer, or neighbor.

I knew I would make new friends in this new life, other women who clipped coupons for baby food and bought diapers by the crate. And I would keep the old friends who were true compatriots—those who are tolerant of my little obsession and patient while I immerse myself in motherhood. Soon enough, Jesse will be off to school, and I will once again have time for and an interest in work, the world, and "the girls."

Month four

BEYOND THE GLASS BUBBLE

You tend to "cocoon" during the first few months of motherhood, deliberately shielding your newborn baby and your own fledgling emotions from the outside world. But there comes a time when the outside world comes knocking loudly and persistently at your door, and there is nothing you can do to keep it out.

Jesse was 4 months old when my father-in-law was diagnosed with inoperable liver cancer. The disease spread quickly, and in three weeks, Harold's father was gone. It seemed so unfair that Jesse would never know either of his grandfathers. My own father had died of lung cancer less than two years before.

The glass bubble that had surrounded our family with the joy of new life was suddenly shattered. Having a baby to care for during this tragedy was in some ways a blessing. No matter what catastrophe has occurred, no matter how badly you want to give into your sorrow, you have a tremendous responsibility that gets you up in the morning and makes you put one foot in front of the other.

And spending the day with a baby who squeals in delight at the sight of your face, and cuddling his warm body at bedtime can banish even the deepest sorrow, at least for a little while.

The day doctors gave us the terrible diagnosis, my mother-in-law spent the night with us. I let her cuddle and play with Jesse long past his normal bedtime. The contact seemed to have a soothing, healing effect.

In the days that followed, as family gathered from all over the country to attend the funeral, Jesse and the other babies in the clan became a balm for the grief we all felt. There was an endless chain of arms eager to hold and cuddle the babies. I don't think they were even put down for naps. They dozed nestled against the soft bosom of an aunt or across the strong forearms of an uncle. You are never more aware of how precious life is than when holding a baby.

ON THE ROAD AGAIN

After the funeral, I felt an urgent need to go home and visit my own family, to see them and touch them and know that they were all right. I wanted to share Jesse with my friends and relatives, and I felt more than a little guilty about having my mother's only grandchild some 2,000 miles away from her.

But I was apprehensive about air travel with a baby. When I thought about the effort it takes just to make a crosstown trip with Jesse, contemplating the logistics of a six-hour flight and a two-week visit at grandma's house was stupefying.

The days of carry-on luggage and spur-of-the-moment

jaunts are gone forever—or at least for the next decade or so. Over the years, I have learned to travel light and had not checked a bag for a flight in years. But on this trip, no matter how I shifted and shuffled the items, I couldn't get everything into two carry-on bags. My necessities took up relatively little space compared to the baby's sleepwear, day outfits, toys, stuffed animals, and books, not to mention the extra diapers, baby food, formula, and bottled water I packed just in case I couldn't get to a grocery store the day we arrived.

So I checked two medium-sized bags and prepared a well-stocked diaper bag for baby items and a backpack for myself, filled with my own can't-do-without-'em items: one change of clothing, an extra pair of shoes, makeup, medicines, and jewelry. Plus a book that I never got a chance to open. If I wasn't occupied with the baby, I was chatting about the baby with other passengers or flight attendants. Traveling with a baby is a great icebreaker. Strangers who normally wouldn't speak to you will ask about your baby and tell you stories about when their children were that age.

I wore a fanny pack that held my wallet, tickets, and other things I needed to keep close at hand. This was more convenient than trying to keep track of a purse. Having only the diaper bag and a backpack to carry left my hands free to maneuver the umbrella stroller, which I couldn't have survived without. It was handy on the trip east to get us quickly from one gate to the next, but it was a life-saver on the return trip, when weather problems stranded us in Dallas, and we stood in line for more than two hours trying to get new tickets. My back would have been permanently strained if I had held Jesse in my arms for that length of time.

When I booked the tickets a couple of weeks in advance, the savvy reservations agent recommended bulkhead rows.

The extra leg room made it much easier to maneuver with the baby. For instance, a bulkhead row will give you plenty of room to get your baby in and out of the stroller without blocking the aisle and holding up a horde of irritable, impatient travelers.

One thing to keep in mind, however, is that bulkhead seats are usually a little more narrow. The trays fit between the seats, since there is no seat in front of you to attach one to, and this takes up an extra inch or two. So, if you haven't lost that pregnancy weight yet, you might need to stick to a regular row. Another disadvantage of the bulkhead seat is that there is no seat in front of you under which you might place a carry-on bag. Everything has to be stowed overhead, which means you'll have to get out of your seat at some point to retrieve the diaper bag. The storage compartments over the bulkhead seat are usually smaller, so if you have two bags and a stroller, you will probably have to grab space in another compartment near you as quickly as possible.

While standing in line on the return trip, I had lots of opportunity to chat with other mothers traveling with their children. One woman complained that she couldn't get her stroller in the compartment above her seat and had to let the flight attendant stow it in another compartment several rows back.

"I had to wait until the plane had emptied so I could backtrack and get the stroller. We almost missed our connecting flight," she said.

For most of the trip, I had a window seat with an empty center seat beside me. Center seats, the ticket agent told me, are usually the last seats to be booked and are, therefore, the most likely to remain empty. The empty seat gave us a little extra room, and the window seat allowed me even more privacy for nursing.

I carefully planned what I would wear on the flight, making sure I had a loose blouse suitable for unobtrusive nursing. There was a spare blouse, appropriately baggy, stuffed into my backpack, just in case of a major mishap. Who wants to smell like sour milk for six hours, especially on an airplane, where at least 50 percent of the air may be recirculated?

Other items I found indispensable for traveling with a baby included disposable bibs and plastic ziplock bags for holding dirty clothing. One thing I wished I had thought to pack was food for myself—crackers and cheese, a granola bar, and some fruit would have come in handy on the return trip. Because of weather and equipment problems, I was only offered pretzels and a beverage twice during the twelve hours it took us to get home. By the end of that ordeal, even Jesse's strained peas were beginning to look good to me. His teething biscuits were not bad—just a little hard to bite into at first. You have to suck on them until they soften up a bit.

Jennifer traveled frequently with her son during his first year, flying back home to Georgia to visit family or to Chicago where her husband was working. One of her observations from these many trips across the country: Flight attendants usually don't offer to help women with a baby or small child, but they are quick to give aid to a man in the same situation.

"It must be the novelty of seeing a man traveling with an infant," she said. Mothers are generally left on their own to fold up the stroller and stow the luggage overhead while balancing a baby on their hip.

On my own trips, I have found the flight attendants and other airport personnel to be friendly and helpful to mothers traveling alone with their children. But there are only a few of them for each 200 to 300 passengers, and you have to be prepared to handle most of the burden without assistance.

Planning ahead and anticipating problems will make it easier. For example, use the rest room in the airport before you depart and between flights. If you are traveling alone, juggling a baby inside the tiny closet on the plane they call a lavatory will be laughably difficult. You can always ask a flight attendant to hold the baby while you go to the bathroom, but you can't guarantee you'll be able to catch one when you need to. I did discover that babies under 5 months old will fit quite comfortably in the lavatory sink. You can hold the baby with one hand while working zippers and snaps with the other.

I was concerned about the change in cabin pressure during takeoffs and landings, so I tried to schedule feedings or give Jesse a sip of juice from a cup during these times. A pacifier may also help. Swallowing, my pediatrician had advised me, opens the eustachian tubes that run from the middle ear to the throat, where a buildup of pressure can be very painful.

It is not a good idea to travel by plane if your baby has a cold, but if you must, check with your pediatrician about using decongestant drops to help keep the baby's ears from becoming blocked.

Despite my apprehension about traveling alone with a baby, I think our first flight went rather well. I just knew that one of his diapers would "explode" during a flight and I'd be stuck in my seat with a mess in my lap, literally.

"I'll never forget the thirteen-hour flight from Sicily," recalled Lynn. "My daughter had diarrhea. When we finally got home to Philadelphia, I swore I'd never travel with a baby again."

I'd also been on many flights where babies cried from takeoff until landing. I was lucky. Jesse slept most of the time and nursed the remainder. If we hadn't had an unex-

pected six-hour layover in Dallas, if the airline hadn't damaged one bag on the way out and "misplaced" one on the
way back, I'd say the trip was a complete success.

At least I'm not afraid to travel with my baby now. If he
can handle all that without throwing a fit, I know we can
handle just about anything. I came much closer to having a
tantrum than he did!

Don't Leave Home Without It

A diaper bag will seem awkward and extraneous in the first
few weeks of motherhood. You may be a bit clumsy as you
try to maneuver this unwieldy apparatus through doorways and along crowded sidewalks. I whacked a few
unsuspecting shoppers and almost wiped out an entire display of china during one of our first outings to the mall.

As the weeks and months pass, however, this cumbersome impedimenta will become just an extra
appendage, as useful and familiar as an old friend. You
may even feel a little naked on those rare occasions when
you go out without bag and baby. Even with a sleek satin
purse tucked under your arm, you'll have this nagging
feeling that something is missing, and you'll check from
time to time to make sure your shoes are on and that you
didn't forget to pull a skirt on over your slip.

Since you're going to become so attached to this baggage, it's a good idea to make sure you choose the right bag for your needs and your own personal style. Many mothers go through several diaper bags before they find the one that is just right for them. Some mothers maintain a supply of bags for different occasions.

The ideal bag is made of an easily cleanable material, has several compartments, and offers both a shoulder strap and short handles for carrying by hand. There should be lots of pockets on the outside for bottles, wipes, and burp cloths, so that you don't have to dig around inside the bag to find these frequently needed items. A changing pad that can be folded and slipped into the diaper bag or an outside pocket is also a must.

There are many sizes and shapes of diaper bags available, from lightweight totes designed for short jaunts to large canvas duffel bags intended for a lengthy journey. When choosing a diaper bag to take along on a trip, make sure it is not too large to be manageable. I purchased a duffel-sized diaper bag that was great for weekend road trips taken in the family car. On an airplane, however, it was too large and bulky to maneuver between the aisles while pushing a baby stroller. Also, I found that the larger the bag, the more you tend to fill it with things that aren't absolutely necessary, an inclination that will leave you with a backache long before you reach your destination.

In chapter 6 I list the items I usually keep packed in our all-day bag and our short-trip bag. The most critical of these items, of course, are the diapers. A general rule of thumb is to pack one diaper for every two hours you will be away from home, plus two just in case you are gone longer than you plan or you have an unexpected explosion.

If you are planning a weekend trip or a longer journey, you should add a first-aid kit to your normal diaper-bag inventory. It should contain any prescription medicines or vitamins your baby is taking, baby acetaminophen, a decongestant, an antiemetic to stop vomiting, an antiperistaltic for diarrhea, and syrup of ipecac to induce vomiting in case of accidental poisoning. Band-Aids, antibacterial cream, tweezers, a thermometer, and individually wrapped alcohol swipes are also good to keep in this bag. Check with your pediatrician for suggestions on other medications and first-aid items to carry with you. Depending on your destination, such additions might include baby sunscreen, insect repellent, calamine lotion, and something to treat allergic reactions to vegetation, insect bites, and stings. Get instructions from your pediatrician on the use of all medications before leaving on your trip.

Another must for the traveling diaper bag is a small purse for your own money, credit cards, and lip gloss. If you just can't squeeze one more item into the diaper bag, consider a backpack, a fanny pack, or a safari jacket with deep pockets for these personal items.

And last but not least, I carry a laminated card with our names and address, our pediatrician's telephone number, my husband's pager number, and a couple of other relatives' telephone numbers to call in case of an emergency. This is a good place to list any allergies or medical conditions your baby may have.

SPILLED MILK

While traveling, I had tried to give Jesse a bottle of formula when it wasn't convenient to breast-feed, such as when we were standing in line with several hundred other stranded passengers. He had something else in mind all together, and lobbed the offending rubber-nippled receptacle and its contents into the next line, where it splattered milk across the pant leg of a briefcase-toting businessman in an expensive-looking suit. Well, he wasn't having a good day anyway. I mouthed an apology, offered the man a wet wipe, and avoided eye contact for the rest of the wait.

By the fourth month, I had become rather protective of my decision to continue breast-feeding. But at this point, I began to regret that I had not introduced a bottle into Jesse's routine before traveling. If I had been giving him an occa-sional bottle at home, he might not have been so quick to reject one when it was necessary.

Most of my baby books, as well as hospital lactation spe-cialists, had warned me that if I waited too long he might not cooperate. They were right.

To be honest, I had been no more eager to give Jesse a supplemental bottle than he was to take one. Four months into motherhood, I wore breast-feeding like a badge of honor, and I was reluctant to give up any of that glory. This was something that only I could do for my baby. No one else could share this part of our lives.

But what if I were sick or injured and couldn't nurse him? Wasn't it about time for me to begin leaving him with someone else for more than an hour? For his benefit, as well as mine, we had to take this step.

When we returned home from our trip, I began to con-sciously make the effort to get him to accept an occasional bottle of formula. While he didn't seem to mind the taste, he almost always rejected the rubber nipples, and each of these attempts became a battle of wills, usually ending with one of us in tears.

After several unsuccessful tries with a standard bottle, I discovered that Jesse might take a few ounces of formula if offered in a cup with a special lid designed for sipping. He was a little young for a sipping cup, and it was messy. Milk would often run out the corners of his mouth, and sometimes he would take too large a swallow and choke. We persevered, and eventually he got the hang of it and was eager to take juice and water from a cup. Formula he would accept with somewhat less enthusiasm.

This success was bittersweet. The good news was that it made him less dependent on me. That was also the bad news.

TABLE MANNERS

Very few people agree on when to begin feeding a baby solid foods. Even fewer agree on which foods to begin with. Our mothers and grandmothers probably fed their babies cereal (they called it pabulum) in the first weeks of life.

One of my sisters-in-law joked (I think) that in her family, newborns were served lasagna to celebrate coming home from the hospital. Many of my friends started cereal at two or three weeks and were absolutely certain that this helped their babies sleep better at night, despite medical research that says this has no effect on sleeping patterns.

It has only been in the last decade or so that pediatricians have cautioned mothers to wait until a baby is at least 4 months old. Some doctors are more adamant about this than others. Research has shown that a very young baby's gastrointestinal tract may not be able to digest solid foods easily.

"The most recent studies indicate that the very early introduction of solid foods may also lead to food allergies later in life," our doctor explained when I pressed for a green light on cereal.

Despite the warnings, I was tempted to introduce solid foods before Jesse's 4-month birthday. I was tantalized by the theory that a little rice cereal at bedtime would make him sleep through the night. After three months of sleepless nights, I was beginning to feel desperate. Coincidentally, he did begin to sleep longer about the time we started cereal, even though the pediatrician said one had nothing to do with the other.

If I had known what changes the introduction of solid food would bring to our lives, I might not have been so eager. I knew it would mean he would begin to nurse less frequently as his intake of solid food increased. What I didn't realize is that I would spend twice as much time trying to get food into him and cleaning up the mess afterward.

And then there were the diapers. Changing a dirty diaper up until this point was not too unpleasant. There was very little odor. In fact, when he was first born, I was certain it smelled a bit like pureed peaches. Harold said this olfactory impression must have been the result of postpartum delirium. Peaches smell like peaches, and poop smells like poop, he said, if not in those exact words.

After we introduced solid foods, diaper changes became a whole new ball game. There was an increase in volume and consistency, and the odor would, I was sure, drive away the neighborhood dogs.

We started with rice cereal mixed with bottled water and a little sugar. (I am, after all, southern, and all southerners sweeten everything, even green beans and sliced tomatoes.) I called my mother to share the experience long-distance with her. Jesse took several spoonfuls and even managed to swallow some of it. It's true, babies do wear more food than they eat!

Later, after Harold got home from work, we tried again, with Daddy doing the feeding. It didn't go quite as well. The baby tried only a couple of tastes before he realized that I was nearby, breasts standing at attention, ready for the evening feeding. He poked out his lower lip and howled like a banshee until I picked him up and offered him the menu he really wanted.

Our first few meals were a challenge of wits and patience. How, my husband wondered, can "one spoonful go in, but two come out?" I was still breast-feeding about every three hours, so I wasn't terribly concerned that he seemed to be wearing more food than he actually swallowed. It was a time of learning for all three of us.

And we had a lot to learn. I had to make sure Jesse was

hungry enough to be interested in cereal but not so hungry that he didn't have the patience to try it. I also had to find the right position. Holding him in my lap wasn't a good idea; my shorts absorbed more food than he did. A "bouncy" seat worked for a while, but soon a high chair was needed.

I had no idea how many shapes and sizes of high chairs there were to choose from. Some tilted or rotated, others attached or rolled or adjusted to different heights. One transformed into a toddler chair and yet another brand could be flipped over and turned into a table and chair. What happened to the simplicity of the old standard wooden high chair with the clamp-on tray? I must have stood in the store for hours gazing at the array before I finally made a decision.

And then there were the feeding utensils. Every manner and shape of spoon, bowl, and cup has been designed to entice the novice mother. My best purchases in this arena were the coated spoon, the easily washed plastic bib with a pocket for crumbs, and the bowl with a hook for your thumb. The hook is not just for looks. It will keep that bowl of sweet potatoes and green peas from being kicked out of your hands and flung against the wall, where it will slither down onto the carpet before you can recover the fumble.

If Jesse didn't like the taste of something, he would let me know by coughing, sputtering, and spitting until the offending matter was splattered randomly over the high chair, the table, the wall, and my lap. The first time I gave him spinach, the expression on his face just before he spit it out reminded me of his father whenever I serve broccoli. This must be what they mean by "spitting image."

If he did like something, he also let me know—by grabbing the bowl and pressing it to his face! Whichever way the wind blew, it was a good idea to have a washcloth or a box of baby wipes within reach. Splat mats and portable vacuum cleaners are also handy at mealtime.

As soon as Jesse was able to sit up in a high chair, I let him join us at the dinner table. In the beginning, this meant that my plate got cold while I tried to funnel the four food groups into a small but quickly moving target. I thought I was doing the right thing by introducing him to the family dinner table at such an early age, but it had taken most of the pleasure out of mealtime for me. I had always enjoyed hot food when it was supposed to be hot and cold food when it was intended to be cold, not vice versa.

It took me almost two months to come up with a better plan: to feed Jesse his dinner first and let him munch on a cracker or teething biscuit while Harold and I enjoyed our meal in relative peace.

Month five

"WORKING" MOMS

New mothers, especially those who had full-time careers before their baby was born, often struggle with feelings of guilt and a sense of insignificance when they choose to stay home during the first year. America has become a two-paycheck society, and women are often made to feel they are not doing their part if they aren't bringing home that second salary.

Simultaneously, mothers who work outside the home must contend with their own guilt demons for sending their child off to be raised by someone else. Fathers get bonuses when they put work before family, but mothers are called overambitious if they do the same.

It is a very confusing time to be a mother. The politically correct responses for working and stay-at-home mothers may be, respectively, "I don't want to work, but I must provide for my child financially" and "I don't want to stay home, but I know it's the best thing for my child." Why can't we just be comfortable saying, "This is what I have chosen to do," and stop worrying about what society expects of us?

The stay-at-home mother and the at-the-office mom are both probably working harder than they ever have at any other time in their life. The at-home mom is often so busy she forgets to eat lunch and may only sit down to feed or play with the baby, but at the end of the day, she thinks she hasn't done anything. She did three loads of laundry before noon, but there were three more piled up on the bedroom floor by nightfall. She made a quick trip to the grocery store and even managed to get dinner prepared without starting any fires or breaking any dishes.

If her husband asks what she did all day, she might just kill him.

I found myself immediately on the defensive whenever some well-meaning acquaintance asked, "You aren't working now, are you?" The term "working mother" implies that women who stay home with their children are not working as hard, that they are perhaps taking the easy road. On the contrary, I found I was working much longer hours than ever before and doing it with a lot less sleep. Sometimes I considered going back to work just so I could get some rest. It might be easier to drop Jesse off at a day-care center and spend the next eight hours concentrating on a job that allowed me time for coffee, lunch, and potty breaks. The motherhood vocation may not offer a regular paycheck, but it is certainly the most demanding occupation I've undertaken, and Jesse is the only boss who has ever insisted on going to the bathroom with me.

When I was working outside the home I had a housekeeper and a lawn-care service. I was on a first-name basis with the staff at most of the local restaurants, and my dry cleaner pressed more of my clothes than I did. Now that I am home with the baby, I feel obligated to do many more household tasks myself.

"I feel like this is a job, and I'm working very hard at it," said Jennifer.

Anne agreed. "This is a twenty-four-hour-a-day job. It never stops. Even when you are sleeping, you are on call." A stay-at-home mom, Anne tries to be supportive of her husband, who often works twelve- and fourteen-hour days. But when he gets home at night and wants to relax, she is ready for a break from baby work and wants someone else to change a diaper or feed her daughter, Tori, the evening meal.

"He is gone so much, and it's just me all day long. I feel like a single mother," she said.

There are times (when the baby is cranky and smears prunes all over the kitchen wall, when a diaper leaks on the freshly cleaned carpet, when I realize I haven't left the house in three days) that I actually miss the mayhem of a busy office, the stress of meeting deadlines, dealing with a lunatic boss, personnel conflicts, equipment problems, staff shortages, or an irate customer. But I wouldn't want to trade all that excitement for seeing my son's first smile and being there to catch him when he takes his first step. I don't want the day-care staff to tell me when he gets his first tooth or speaks his first word. I don't want to learn about these milestones secondhand. My feelings may change as time passes, but so far I have wanted to be there for every achievement. But that is not the answer for all women.

Many mothers go back to work as soon as possible for financial reasons, while others simply need to get back to the real world, to have that connection with other adults. Whatever decision a woman makes about her career, she should not feel guilty. Guilt is our own worst enemy. We must continually remind ourselves that what's best for Mommy is probably what's best for baby, too. A contented mother is more likely to have a contented child.

"I think it makes a better kid," said Lisa, a stockbroker who returned to work when her daughter Alexis was 6 weeks old. "When a mother works, her kids have to learn to cope with change, to be independent. They learn they can be cared for by somebody else, they can sleep in somebody else's bed. It doesn't always have to be their own. I think a working mother raises a stronger child."

Alexis also attends "mother's day out" (a few hours of free baby-sitting offered by a local church) once a week so she can socialize with other children. "This gives her a break in the routine. It's not the same old song and dance," Lisa said. She wants her daughter to be exposed to a wide variety of experiences so that she will be "a more well-rounded" child.

"During the week, Grandpa sometimes takes her to visit one of his friends who lives on a farm. If she was home with me, the chances are slim to none that we would do that. I might take her to the zoo, but not a farm where she could actually touch the animals," she said.

Lisa returned to work because of financial necessity, but she said she would have gone back whether she needed to or not.

"I love my work. I looked forward to going back, and I was ready for a break from the baby routine," she said. "Naturally, I had some regrets, some maternal guilt. I gave birth to this child, but someone else was going to raise her, see her first smile, be there when she rolled over or crawled for the first time."

Lisa found a workable solution to the problem of missing all those firsts: She simply asked her mother-in-law,

Alexis's caregiver for most of the week, not to tell her when the baby reached a new level of development.

"That way, when I saw her do something, I thought it was the very first time. It's all a mind game," Lisa said.

For Lisa, the most difficult aspect of being a working mother is scheduling. "A child needs a routine, and that is hard to establish when you don't have set working hours. I have to work when it is convenient for the client. Some days I go home at five. Some days I leave work at five, rush to pick her up, drop her off at home with her daddy, and go back to work."

And then there are the sleepless nights.

"You can't be up all night and then come to work and function well the next day," she said, adding that she probably loses more "battles of will" with her daughter because it means they will all get more sleep.

"I made a mistake in the beginning that I'm paying for now. I always let her fall asleep in my arms after eating. Now, I have to hold her or rock her until she goes to sleep or she screams," Lisa said.

"I'm glad I'm working, but sometimes it's really hard. You come home in the afternoon, and you're tired, your child is tired, and it's a struggle," Lisa said. "You just want to scream, but you have to tell yourself to stay calm and things will go much more smoothly."

Many of the new mothers I meet today are trying to have the best of both worlds—staying home with their children and earning a paycheck. Working part-time or flexible hours or doing free-lance work from their home are some of the options. Many of the writers I have worked with at various newspapers around the country have found part-time and free-lance work to be a creative compromise.

"I love working, and I do miss the camaraderie, the

jokes, what's going on in the world," said Tammy, who decided not to return to her full-time job as a newspaper reporter after her son, Scott, was born. "But I keep my hand in by working free-lance projects and writing a column every week. My mind is only partially turned to mush by listening to Barney (a television dinosaur popular with children) all day."

Tammy said she works anywhere from two to twenty hours a week, and when she has a major project deadline approaching, she gets extra help from her husband, David.

"I have a really supportive husband. He does all the cooking," she said.

Along with writing a weekly newspaper column and doing other periodic free-lance jobs, Tammy was working twenty hours a week for a local university, until the pressure got to be too much.

"Somebody called in the middle of pancakes. I don't cook, and I was having to read the directions and try to answer questions over the phone. It just made me crazy, so I quit the university job. It was just too much with a baby at home," she said.

Much of her work is done by telephone, and she uses "mother's day out" two days a week for interviews and other tasks that must be done in person. "Sometimes I'll be doing an interview over the phone with *Willy Wonka and the Chocolate Factory* playing in the background. Once I was interviewing the dean of education at the university while pulling Scott out of the toilet. You just have to hope that they can't hear what's going on.

"I would probably feel a lot calmer if I were back at work," she said.

There are other drawbacks to working at home with a child underfoot, Tammy said. You have to deal with perceptions. "People think you lay around all day, watching soaps. It used to really bother me when someone would ask for my work number and I would say, 'It's my home number,' and they would look at me funny, or at least I thought they did. It doesn't bother me so much anymore."

The hardest part of being a work-at-home mother is finding the motivation and getting organized, said Tracy, a realtor who decided to work from her home after her son, Nathan, was born. "I thought I could work from my home and take care of Nathan, but I can't do it if he's here, so he goes to a sitter three days a week."

Tracy said she makes up for lost time on her workdays by starting early and going nonstop until it's time to pick up her son at the baby-sitter's.

"That's the only way I can make it. I didn't expect that motherhood would be so demanding physically, that he would be so busy and active and need so much attention," Tracy said. "When he's at the sitter's, he gets the attention he needs, and I can get some work done."

Jesse was only a few weeks old when I accepted the first postbaby free-lance assignment. I had not planned to work until he was at least 3 months old, but I had done several projects for this company in the past and never was very good at saying no.

It took me three days to do what normally would have taken one focused afternoon. I could make a telephone call or two, maybe work fifteen or twenty minutes before I had to stop to fetch a dropped toy, change a diaper, or feed him.

I thought it would get easier as time passed. By the fifth month, I had hoped to be working at least four hours a day, four or five days a week. As anticipated, Jesse was not nursing quite as often and did not require nearly as many diaper and clothing changes as he had during the first four months.

But this didn't mean, as I had predicted, that he demanded any less of my time or energy. In the early months, he only needed the basics—food, shelter, and a clean diaper. At five months, he needed these things in smaller doses but wanted much larger helpings of my companionship and attention.

His daytime naps had become short, infrequent, and unpredictable. He did not just cry for me to feed him or change his diaper. He demanded to be entertained! I would put him down on the floor of my office and surround his play mat with brightly colored or musical toys. This would last for a few minutes, until he threw them all out of reach.

I would stop to fetch the toys, then try to resume work, as soon as I could remember what exactly I had been doing. A few more minutes would pass before he would grow bored with his selection of teething rings, singing balls, and squeaking teddy bears, fix me with an intent stare, and scream, "ga!" until I abandoned my computer and dropped to the floor to play with him.

After several weeks of this, I realized my home-office arrangement wasn't working. I loved spending time with Jesse at this age. His world was expanding, and he was infinitely curious about everything he could see, hear, touch, and, especially, taste. It was a constant distraction, and I knew my writing career would flounder completely if I didn't arrange for some sort of child care. How could I be expected to write brilliantly creative prose with a baby chewing on my ankles?

A Pair of Au Pairs, Please

"Hire a baby-sitter," my mother advised.

Easier said than done. How could I find anyone who could care for him as well as I do? After five months of being his primary caretaker, I was convinced only I could change his diaper, read to him, or soothe his tears when he was tired and needed a nap. I just knew he wouldn't be safe with anyone else. I was barely comfortable leaving him alone with his father for a half hour or so while I went to the grocery store. How could I possibly leave him with a stranger?

Ideally, your mother or mother-in-law is the best possible choice. Their values and ideas about child rearing are probably very close to your own, and you know they would protect and care for your child with unconditional love. Unfortunately, our society has become rather transient, and many new mothers find themselves living far away from the typical family support system. My own mother lives 2,000 miles away, and my mother-in-law, recently widowed, was visiting relatives in another state.

"I had always had my mother to watch Jenna," said Shelley, who moved away from her hometown for the first time when her husband accepted a job transfer.

Shelley said she "felt really strange and apprehensive" about calling complete strangers, people who had advertised in the local newspaper's classified section. But she carefully checked all their references and did lengthy personal interviews.

I had hired a baby-sitter on only a few rare occasions during the first few months. But Harold was always home for at least part of those evenings, so I didn't feel quite as much anxiety about leaving. On my first ladies' night out, I only called home twice in three hours.

"I think we've had a baby-sitter four times in a year," Chalene said. "If we couldn't take Skyler with us, we just didn't go."

When Chalene's father was ill, she left Skyler at her sister's house and spent most of the day at the hospital.

"He was perfectly fine all day, a little angel. But at night, as soon as I picked him up, he was cranky," she recalled. "It was as if he was mad at me for leaving him, and he was going to make me pay for it."

Like finding a new doctor or dentist, choosing a baby-sitter is not an easy task. How would I ever find someone who was responsible, warm, and loving, who would provide stimulating play, comfort his boo-boos with a kiss, and change his diaper often enough to prevent diaper rash? And who didn't have a police record?

I began the search by visiting day-care centers in our neighborhood and checking out advertisements in the Yellow Pages and newspapers for in-home child care. The child-care centers were bright and clean, and the nanny services offered professionals with excellent training and references, along with full background checks. But my salary as a free-lance writer didn't justify the expense of either one.

Child care in a private home was cheaper, but I was uncomfortable leaving a baby with a single adult surrounded by three or four toddlers, who could pinch, poke, and prod all of his vulnerable soft spots, as well as pass on cold and flu viruses.

One by one, I was eliminating the possibilities, and I began to despair of ever finding someone suitable. Finally, a neighbor introduced me to a retired grandmother who was willing to come to my home. This seemed to offer the most advantages. Jesse would be in familiar surroundings, and I could look in on him from time to time.

If you can't find a grandmother surrogate, a young teenager might be a good choice for the after-school hours, especially if you are going to be at home the entire time. A teenager will need closer supervision but will be more easily molded into the type of baby-sitter you want. Sometimes the "grandmothers" have preconceived notions about baby care that don't match your own philosophies.

For example, Betty was a delightful older woman who believed a baby should never be allowed to cry, so she would hold him for hours, even while he slept. Her arms would grow numb, but she would not budge him. It was comforting to know that he was being cared for so lovingly, but after Betty went home, he expected me to hold him constantly, too. With some gentle prodding from me, she did begin to put him into his playpen for naps.

It's wise to have at least two or three baby-sitters who are familiar with you and your baby. The good ones are hard to find and are often booked weeks in advance. Getting referrals from other mothers, unless they were past the baby-sitter stage, was like pulling teeth. No one wants to share her coveted roster of tried and tested baby-sitters.

"Please don't call mine," Jennifer pleaded when I mentioned that I was looking for another backup sitter. It had taken her almost a year to find someone she was comfortable leaving her son with, and she didn't want to have to make reservations a month in advance.

I know exactly how she felt. Only torture would make me reveal my own sources.

Leaving your baby with a sitter does get a little easier with each outing. Eventually, you stop anticipating disaster each time you leave the house without him.

Then, just about the time you have gotten over your nail biting, it hits you that your baby has very easily come to love a new special person in his life. Now it's time to deal with jealousy and your own separation anxiety.

I am embarrassed to admit how much it bothered me the first time Jesse beamed a brilliant smile at his sitter and held out his arms for her to take him from me. I didn't want him to cry or be distressed while I was gone, but, darn it all, couldn't he have waited until after I left to chew on another woman's face? (This seems to be how he shows affection: growling and biting a chin, nose, or cheek. Perhaps he's spending a little too much time with the dog.)

Month six

A Day in the Life of Supermom

Faster than a speeding bullet, able to leap tall buildings . . . It's not a bird. It's not a plane. It's the mother of a 6-month-old baby—a woman who flies through her day with the speed of light and the boundless energy of Supermom. Only kryptonite or perhaps a glass of Zinfandel at the end of the day will slow her down.

There are a great many buzzwords in the mothering business today. I have yet to meet a first-time mother who doesn't know exactly what I mean when I say "superwoman syndrome." Most of us feel compelled to be everything we were before—career woman, chef, laundress, housekeeper, grocery shopper, bookkeeper, chauffeur, gofer—and a mother besides.

By the end of the year, I had learned to let the dishes pile up in the sink when necessary and to turn a blind eye when the dust bunnies propagated under the bed. But six months into motherhood, I was still trying to live up to impossible ideals and was constantly frustrated that although I was doing the best I could, I never quite seemed to catch up.

I have always been compulsively neat. When my mother comes to visit, she torments me by moving my knickknacks around a little bit, maybe just an inch or two out of place. Then she sits back and waits to see how long it takes me to notice and reposition them.

An uncluttered kitchen, a floor that always looks just vacuumed, a coffee table with carefully arranged magazines— these are all memories in the dusty rafters of my postpartum mind. Baby bottles, bibs, bowls, and other feeding paraphernalia now cover every inch of counter space in my kitchen. Each room has an overflowing basket of toys, and the family room is crowded with the required playpen, swing, bouncy seat and exercise saucer, a replacement for the old-fashioned walker. The magazines and books on the coffee table have all been chewed on. I don't think *Southern Living* magazine will be calling for a photo shoot anytime soon.

Once, this mayhem would have bothered me. But much to my surprise, I have found myself enjoying the sight of my son crumpling the pages of my newest magazines and turning over the wastebasket so he could pilfer through the junk mail. However, I do still pick up all the toys and straighten the family room every night after I put the baby to bed. Somehow this gives me the illusion of some measure of control over my new environment. And it helps to begin the next day with a head start on housecleaning.

Life had become chaotic, yes, but halfway through the first year, we had developed a somewhat relaxed schedule. Within wide parameters, I knew what to expect when it came to feeding, napping, and diapers. But like many new moms, at the end of the day, I often wondered what I had accomplished. Against the advice of other moms, who said, "You'll be better off not knowing," I decided to chronicle a typical day. Here's what it was like.

6:00 A.M.:   Coffee, cereal, and the morning paper.

6:30 A.M.:   Baby wakes and nurses for half an hour.

7:00 A.M.:   Playtime with books and "developmental" toys that rattle, squeak, or can be pulled along by a string.

8:00 A.M.:   Breakfast of little champions—cereal and fruit—followed by a bath and diaper change.

9:00 A.M.:   Breast-feed ten to fifteen minutes. If baby takes a nap, I use this time to clean up breakfast items, put the house in order, or do a little yard work, baby monitor strapped to my waist.

11:00 A.M.:   Baby wakes and may play quietly in his crib until he sees or hears me nearby.

11:30 A.M.:   Time for a diaper change, followed by lunch—a fruit he eats with relish and some sort of vegetable that I have to spend a half hour coercing him to swallow, washed down by a little breast milk.

12:30 P.M.:   Fix my own lunch, grab a quick shower while baby plays (or screams) in his playpen, then it's time to hit the road, with stops at the grocery store, dry cleaners and one-hour photo shop, where I have reached frequent-shutter status.

3:00 P.M.:   I rush home with just enough time to nurse the baby, put away the groceries,

	do some laundry, pay the bills, take out the garbage, and start dinner.
6:00 P.M.:	Nurse the baby while finishing dinner preparations.
7:00 P.M.:	Dinner at last. A spoonful for baby, a forkful for me, a spoonful for baby, a forkful for me . . .
7:30 P.M.:	Clean up the kitchen, fold some clothes, and sort through the day's mail, while Daddy plays with baby.
8:00 P.M.:	Sit down to visit with hubby for a while.
8:30 P.M.:	Get baby ready for bed—fresh diaper, footed sleep suit, clean hands and face.
9:00 P.M.:	Nurse for thirty to forty minutes, until baby falls asleep, then carry him upstairs and slip him into his crib.
10:00 P.M.:	Pick up toys, crawl up the stairs, and collapse into bed.

And you get up the next day and repeat the process. It sounds exhausting because it is, but what gets left out of such a cut-and-dried recording is the fun you have watching your baby as he begins to explore the world and the joy you feel whenever he smiles at you or holds his arms out to be picked up.

Six months is such an exciting stage of infancy. Perhaps what I learned the most from recording my day was that I needed to slow down a little and enjoy it more. I realized that I was getting so wrapped up in daily chores that I was not fully aware of how much fun it could be just to watch my baby as he learned to roll and creep and babble.

Recording my activities also gave me some insight into

how I could better organize my day, so maybe it was a good idea after all.

When I worked full-time in a newspaper office, I was used to being up and out of the house by 6:30 or 7 A.M., but in the first six months of motherhood, I seemed to have lost control of the mornings. Like many first-time mothers, I found it would be noon or later before I had a shower and fixed my face.

After studying the schedule of a typical day, I decided to forgo the morning newspaper so that I could shower before Jesse woke up. I could sip that first glorious cup of coffee while putting on a face and getting dressed for the day.

I also learned that waiting until midafternoon to run errands and then trying to do them all at once made for a nerve-racking, virtually impossible task that would leave me completely frazzled by the time dinner was ready. Grocery shopping and other errands turned out to be much easier in the mornings, when stores were less crowded and traffic not as heavy. And Jesse was more apt to nap in the car during the cool morning hours. Sometimes I would break the day up, doing some errands in the morning and others in the afternoon. This seemed much less disruptive of the baby's schedule and left me with a little more energy at the end of the day.

By six months, I had become a pro at shopping with a baby. I kept two diaper bags ready to go at all times. The large one was for all-day trips and contained a day's supply of diapers and wipes, jars of baby food and juice, water, toys, a bib, two burp rags, a receiving blanket, and a change of clothing. As baby gets older, it's wise to add crackers, cookies, and bite-sized cereal to the all-day bag.

The second bag was considerably smaller, intended only for short shopping trips of one to two hours. It held only a few diapers, wipes, juice, water, a burp rag, and a couple of chewable, squeaky toys. I usually kept the smaller bag in the car. That way I never forgot to take it with us, and I never had to make a trip back into the house to get it after I already had the baby strapped into his car seat.

If you take a few minutes a couple of times a week to replenish both bags and keep them ready to go, it will save a lot of time whenever you have to leave the house, especially if it is a spur-of-the-moment excursion.

Jennifer, who had become one of my mentor moms, also advised me to "always take a diaper bag in with you, even when you know you'll just be a minute." It's inevitable, she said, that when you're not prepared is exactly when you'll wish you were. How right she was.

I was looking for a blouse, a specific color and style, when I saw the 40 Percent Off sign. It would only take a few minutes to check out the sale rack, so I decided we wouldn't need a diaper bag. I made a quick find and was standing in line to make my purchase when I heard the spinach Jesse had for lunch coming up. It doesn't sound any better than it looks. He was bent over the strap of his umbrella stroller trying to "pick" the flowers off the carpet. I guess the strain was a little too much on a full stomach, especially one full of something that smelled so nasty.

Supermom would have whipped a bottle of carpet cleaner and a baby wipe out of her gilded holster and cleaned up the mess without blinking an eye. Red-faced, I took my change and made a quick getaway, vowing never again to shop unarmed.

Another bit of advice from Jennifer: Choose stores with shopping carts. Babies in strollers can't see you or interact with you and will get bored and fussy much quicker, she said. Her final word of advice on shopping with a baby, especially an active one who has begun to crawl or walk: "Don't. Just don't go," she said. "You can't keep him in the stroller. He is too busy. We used to be able to take Collin out to eat. Those days are gone. I'm not sure when they'll be back."

Shopping with a baby is a science, an art form that requires skill, technique, craftiness, and planning—maybe even a little prestidigitation. Another task requiring a touch of magic after baby arrives is laundry. What I once took for granted now requires a new talent for juggling a dozen balls in the air at one time, then making them all disappear.

THE SPIN CYCLE

How can something so small create so much laundry? In a single day, I might wash the crib sheets and blankets because a diaper leaked, an adorable baby outfit now covered in cereal, and a sweater splattered with mashed mango. (A word of advice here: If the baby sneezes while eating, duck for cover, unless you like being showered with food.) Later, I would add to the laundry pile the jeans I was wearing when he spit up in my lap, the quilt he was lying on when yet another diaper exploded, a couple of bibs, and some washcloths.

And my husband expected to have *his* underwear washed and socks matched up and arranged in the proper drawer?

But take heart. It does get better. Toward the end of the sixth month, almost overnight, Jesse's diapers ceased leaking with such frequency, and he stopped spitting up almost constantly. I don't know if I finally found the right type of diaper, or if he simply grew to fit them better.

Do We Have Containment?

During the first six months, we sampled a wide variety of disposable diapers in an attempt to find one that would contain both liquid and solid matter. Time turned out to be the only solution. As Jesse became more mobile and spent less time lying on his back and side, the leaking decreased, and as he ate more solid food, his stool became much less fluid and less likely to overflow.

Thank goodness mothers today have a choice in diapers. I never really considered anything but disposable diapers, though I felt a little guilty at choosing what seemed to be the easy way out. I couldn't forget hearing my mother speak with a certain pride of soaking, washing, and boiling cloth diapers when my brother and I were babies. As if the more difficult the task, the better it must be for Baby.

Cloth diapers are cheaper, if you do not consider the value of the time it takes to clean them, and are more ecologically responsible. You can cut down on some of the work involved with cloth diapers by using a home-delivery diaper service.

You will hear a great deal of conflicting advice concerning cloth and disposable diapers. Cloth diaper services often boast of fewer incidences of diaper rash, but so do the manufacturers of superabsorbent disposable diapers. The answer to the diaper rash dilemma seems to lie not necessarily in the type of diaper used but in how the diaper is used. The best way to avoid irritation is to change the diaper often—every hour or two for newborns and every few hours for older babies and always immediately after any bowel movement.

Something else I learned in the early months was not to stock up on disposable diapers in the infant and small sizes. Jesse outgrew these sizes so quickly I ended up giving away diapers I had bought by the case. Once he had reached the "stage three" size—usually sixteen to twenty-four pounds—his growth was not so dramatic, and I was able to purchase diapers in bulk at a better price.

When Jesse was a newborn, we went through ten or twelve diapers in a single day. At six months, that number was cut in half, but diapers were still a critically important part of his ever-changing wardrobe. In six months, his attire had evolved from drawstring gowns and footed sleepers to pullover shirts and overalls. I still preferred the one-piece outfits with wide necks and snaps at the crotch.

A well-meaning but childless friend sent us an adorable little designer outfit as a baby gift when Jesse was born. Unfortunately, it had a turtleneck and a zipper down the back—no snaps. It was such a struggle to get him into and out of the little suit that it hung in the closet until he outgrew it. It was his cutest outfit, but you have to consider comfort and convenience first when buying baby clothes.

Rarely do mothers today limit their babies to the traditional ice-cream parlor pastels. Park days are an explosion of primary colors in styles that often mimic the parents' own tastes. At six months, Jesse's wardrobe was a rainbow of blues, greens, yellows, and reds. My own wardrobe, however, had become somewhat neglected.

From Best-Dressed
to Dressed for a Mess

How do you spot a brand-new mother? She's the one in the dingy, stained, smelly sweat pants, carrying the child in the Baby Dior suit with the Armani booties and the Gucci rattle.

I found comfort in my oldest, most worn (and most unflattering) sweat suits and T-shirts. It's not that I had ceased to care what I looked like, but I'd grown weary of seeing my best clothes get peed on, spit up on, and splattered with oatmeal.

On a rare dress-up occasion, I was meeting a friend at the mall. I had this picture-perfect vision of how we would look oh-so-fashionable as we strolled our adorable, quiet little babies, window shopped, and talked about motherhood. I was wearing a new silk blouse and matching slacks. I decided to "tank" Jesse up with a little cereal and fruit before we left, so he wouldn't get hungry during our outing. We were on our last spoonful when something—it could have been that the previous spoonful went up his nose rather than into his mouth—caused him to sneeze. White clumps intermingled with bright orange splashed across my elegant, sophisticated black outfit. I looked like a living canvas for a Picasso wannabe.

I didn't have time to change, so I leaned over the sink, hosed off my blouse, and drove with the window down so I could air dry on the way to the mall. Now I know the true meaning of wash-and-wear clothing: something you can wash while still wearing it.

Perhaps it is a good idea to wait until the last possible moment to get dressed, or don't get "dressed" at all— go casual.

Living with a baby means you have to get used to a certain amount of mess and disarray (*mayhem* might be a better word). It means you have to be able to forgive yourself for not putting on any makeup. At least you washed your face and brushed your teeth, didn't you?

I must admit, though, that on occasion, I did get a little lax with my personal grooming.

"You have something on your face," my husband said, backing up ever so slightly. Jesse was 6 months old. It could have been anything.

"What is it?" I queried.

"I can't tell." He backed a little farther away.

"What color is it?" I pressed.

"I can't tell."

"Well, can you get it off?" I was getting a little exasperated.

"I don't think so," he said, still backing.

My husband is a brave man. I'm sure he wouldn't hesitate to flick a spider from my shoulder or swat a bee out of my hair. He might even leap into the street to snatch me out of the path of a speeding bus. He has always been my paladin. But touching unidentifiable baby stuff is, apparently, out of the question for even the most stalwart knight.

I took a long look at myself in the mirror and decided it was time to clean up my act. I went shopping the next day and bought new play clothes. I threw the sweat pants away (I considered a ceremonial burning but was afraid that might require a special city permit) and promised myself that my hair would always be washed and brushed, if not styled, and that my face, if not painted, would at least be clean.

MOTHER TOLD YOU SO

Keeping my face clean was always a task my mother stressed as being of utmost importance. Up there right along with wearing clean underwear in case you're in an accident. (Thank God, the only time I was in an accident I was actually wearing underwear.)

I guess a lot of things my mother told me are surfacing from my deep subconscious these days. You never really understand those maternal admonitions until you become a mother yourself. Those words that seemed like alarmist forebodings now ring of wise counsel. ("You'll put your eye out with that" comes immediately to mind.)

Sometimes I have to take a quick look over my shoulder just to see if Mom is there—the words coming out of my mouth sound so much like her own. These are always words of caution. Motherhood can turn even the cockiest daredevil into a scaremonger. This is instinctive, but you can't let it get out of hand. It is wise to be cautious about the dangers of the world, but you shouldn't waste your energy worrying about all the things you can't control. Let your mother worry about that.

Writing about my mother is not easy. She is a generous woman who loves her family above all else. Presenting her with a grandchild was the greatest gift I could have ever given her, but his birth did put a temporary strain on our mother-daughter relationship in those early months.

"Many of the people I see are in conflict with their mothers," said Laguna Hills psychotherapist Helen Greenblatt, Ph.D. "Past conflicts with mothers often resurface when a woman has her own children."

Grandparents, she said, often stake a claim of ownership over a new baby, particularly if it is a first grandchild. Even though I had read about this and talked with other mothers about their experiences, I wasn't fully prepared for how I felt when my own mother began to lay claim to my newborn son.

When she called him "my baby" and said she wanted to take him home with her, it was almost impossible for me to conceal my own feelings of possessiveness.

"This is a very normal feeling, especially with a first baby. It's a power play," Dr. Greenblatt explained. "Your mother missed a once in a lifetime opportunity to praise you for a job well done and to give you possession of your child. She should have enjoyed her grandchild as an extension of her child."

When a situation like this occurs, Dr. Greenblatt said, a new mother need not banish her mother, but she should communicate her discomfort.

"Respect your own feelings. If you need to be possessive, do so in a gentle way. Establish the boundaries," she said.

"Brand-new moms often tell their mothers they don't want them to come visit for two or three weeks, so that they can bond privately with their baby. When the second child is born, however, those same mothers are asking their moms to come right away."

A new, first-time mother may also be feeling very unsure of herself, uncertain of her abilities and worried that her baby will not love her, Dr. Greenblatt said.

"You don't have to worry about the baby loving grandmother more than mother. That child knows who its mother is," she said.

"You have to keep the lines of communication open when Grandma comes to stay after the baby is born. If there is a misunderstanding, don't go off in a huff. If your mother says something that hurts you, ask her why she said such a thing. Maybe there's a deeper reason, something that needs to be resolved, so you can both go on with your lives," Dr. Greenblatt continued.

"Voice your concerns. She'll understand. She was a new mom once herself, you know," she added.

My mother's help was invaluable, but there were times when I simply needed to do things myself, perhaps just to prove that I could. Even if I was floundering in a sea of baby tears, I still needed to have control of the ship, to be plotting my own course. This must be hard for any well-meaning grandmother to understand, especially when she still sees her daughter as her own baby.

I've heard many first-time mothers complain that their own moms continue to view them as children, no matter what their age, and just can't believe they can be responsible or experienced enough to care for a baby.

I must admit to feeling somewhat insulted when Mother commented that my brother and I never cried when we were babies. Didn't that mean I must be doing something wrong if my baby cried? Later, when I had time to think it through, I realized that my mother probably just didn't remember how much her children cried. Mothers tend to forget the bad times and remember only the good things about their babies.

"My mother raised four children, but I found myself telling her how to hold the baby for feeding and reminding her to burp," said Gayle, a mother of twins. "I had no experience at this, but I felt that only I knew what was best for my babies."

Most new mothers today have read so many books and magazine articles on child care that we feel like experts by proxy. Our mothers weren't inundated with all this literature but somehow managed to rear us and our siblings on nothing but the sage advice of their mothers and grandmothers. My guess is, they probably resented their mother's advice, too.

"When my own children quote to me from those expert baby books, I just heave a sigh of resignation and tell myself to keep my mouth shut," said Dr. Greenblatt, who presents workshops and speaks to various groups on what she calls her favorite subject, the mother–daughter relationship.

Even though we disagreed on some things (such as hand washing and ironing all of the baby clothes), I found that my mother and I shared a lot of beliefs concerning baby care. It had been more than thirty years since she'd had a baby in her house, but some of the basics never change. No matter what trend in baby care the experts are promoting today, loving, rocking, and singing nursery rhymes remain constant through the generations.

A grandmother's advice shouldn't be ignored, even if you choose not to follow it, Dr. Greenblatt said. The important thing, she added, is to keep the relationship from becoming a power struggle, with your new baby as the pawn.

Once we had gotten past the rocky beginning, Jesse's birth seemed to draw me closer to my mother in many ways. I have a new appreciation of the sacrifices in time, energy, and money that she and my father made. I suppose, like most daughters, I will always be seeking her approval in all the things I do, including motherhood. I felt I had "arrived" on one visit home when I overheard her telling a friend that I was "such a good mother." I just tried to ignore the note of genuine surprise in her voice.

TAKING INVENTORY

When Jesse was almost 7 months old, I undertook an act of true courage. I pulled all of my prepregnancy blue jeans out of the closet and tried them on. Out of a dozen or so pairs, there were only three that I couldn't zip even lying down with my feet up in the air (contrary to popular opinion, reversing gravity apparently doesn't help relocate fatty tissue). Despite those few uncooperative pairs, I felt pretty good about myself.

My doctor was right when she said I would feel more like my old self at six months. I was almost back to my prepregnancy size (if not exactly the same shape), and I no longer felt as if my insides were about to fall out. While my blouses still didn't fit (and probably won't until I stop breast-feeding), the rest of my clothes were more comfortable.

I took a complete inventory of myself at about this time, checking out my hair and skin with a rather critical eye. For six months, I had been so busy trying to get a handle on this motherhood business that I had paid little attention to myself beyond the most obvious physical requirements.

At six months, I still had a couple of small brown spots on my face, but they seemed to be fading. Many of the skin problems commonly associated with pregnancy—acne, dark patches, moles, and spidery blood vessels—will disappear in three to six months after delivery.

Hormones are almost always the culprit behind these pregnancy-related skin conditions. Fluctuating estrogen and progesterone levels can do much more than make your moods swing. This can also alter sebaceous-gland activity. It gives some women the perfectly clear skin they have always longed for but leaves others with an outbreak of acne reminiscent of those pubescent preteen days.

Dr. Alexander Miller, a California dermatologist, says hormones don't actually cause these skin disorders but can trigger them, or "facilitate" their occurrence, by making the skin more receptive. Heredity is also a factor in how pregnancy will affect a woman's skin before and after her baby is born.

Acne that persists long after delivery can be treated with benzoyl peroxide gel, Retin-A, or oral antibiotics. "We treat postpartum acne the same way we treat normal, nonpregnancy-related acne," Dr. Miller says.

Treatments, however, are sometimes postponed until after the baby is weaned if the mother is breast-feeding. Although benzoyl peroxide and Retin-A are not known to cause problems in breast-fed babies, some doctors advise waiting just to be on the safe side. Also, antibiotics can cause diarrhea in some breast-fed babies.

Rashes and itchy, dry skin are other problems that often plague women during pregnancy, but these, too, almost always disappear soon after delivery.

Throughout pregnancy I experienced patches of "capillary spiders" on my cheeks. One was very prominent, especially in the last month. It was still visible at six months postpartum but was much smaller and less red, except when I became overheated or emotional. Then it would become much too obvious to conceal with makeup.

These spiders, also known as vascular clumps, occur when changes in estrogen levels cause new blood vessels to be formed and existing ones to dilate. If these clusters don't disappear after delivery, they can be removed by cauterization or laser treatments. Of the two, cauterization costs considerably less, but laser treatments are usually more effective, especially with larger clusters.

I waited until Jesse was 9 months old to have my own "vascular blush" removed. I felt a twinge of guilt at being such a victim of my own vanity, especially since the vessels were so small. But it made me feel a little more attractive and boosted my self-confidence. It's so easy during your first year of motherhood to ignore your own needs, especially the insignificant little vanities. But treating yourself, stroking your own ego from time to time, will do wonders to revitalize your spirit and make you a better mother in the process.

Other legacies of pregnancy that remained with me at six months were moles and freckles that appeared on my legs and arms. Some of them were preexisting but had become larger and darker during pregnancy. A few of the moles disappeared on their own within a few months, but many of the freckles seem to be here to stay.

One of the moles looked a bit suspicious, and the dermatologist recommended I have it removed. During the procedure, the medical student who was assisting complimented me on how calm I was and how still I laid upon the operating table. "I'm sort of enjoying this," I said to her. "It's the most rest I've had in months."

Other women I spoke with during the year reported patches of dark skin on their face, particularly around the eyes, forehead, nose, cheeks, and upper lip. Melasma, also referred to as "the mask of pregnancy" or "mother's mask," usually goes away after hormones have returned to their normal levels, according to Dr. Miller.

"But this may take some time. After all, these conditions did not develop overnight," he says, adding that he usually advises new mothers to "be patient" and wait at least a year before considering drastic measures, such as surgery or laser treatments, to eliminate pregnancy-related skin conditions.

In the meantime, for those who no longer have any patience, a combination of bleaching creams, sunscreen, and Retin-A treatments can often help speed the process of elimination for these unsightly skin spots.

Hair loss is another complaint of many new mothers. I did not experience the hair loss that so many women do two to four months following the birth of a child, but I had stocked up on detangler and conditioner before the birth, and these products helped to keep me from tugging unnecessarily on those tender locks. My hair, however, did darken in color, becoming much more red than blond, and seemed much drier and more brittle. I did notice slightly more hair loss later in the year, after I stopped taking prenatal vitamins.

Again, time is the best cure for postpartum hair loss, Dr. Miller said. Also, he said, postpartum women don't actually lose as much hair as they think they do. Hormonal changes during pregnancy slowed down normal hair loss, leaving their tresses thicker and more luxuriant than ever before. After delivery, normal loss resumes, and most of the hair not shed during pregnancy falls out in the first few months. New growth can't keep up, and hair appears thinner for a time.

A new haircut, perhaps a shorter style, or frequent trims on your usual do will help until the end of the year, when hair should be back to its prepregnancy condition.

Taking Care of Yourself

Self-neglect seems to be the common thread that runs through the lives of many first-time mothers. We are so concerned with the health, safety, and development of our child and the integration of a new baby into our family lifestyle that we often forget to tend to our own needs. The first place this neglectfulness will show is the face.

Many first-time mothers complain about their complexion following the birth of a child, but facialist Nicole Koob said there are many things a new mother can do to give her face a lift without resorting to surgery. Here are a few of her suggestions:

- Eat healthy foods and resist the urge to indulge in sweets.

- Drink plenty of water.

- Relax whenever possible and get as much sleep as you can.

- Periodically treat your face to a deep cleansing and exfoliation to get rid of dead skin cells.

- Keep your face clean and well nourished with a good moisturizer (that means don't go to bed with out washing your face and covering it with lotion, no matter how tired you are).

- Treat yourself to a professional facial. Not only will it be good for your skin but it will ensure you at least an hour of total relaxation.

BACK TALK

Another physical malady often overlooked as the result of your new status as a mother is the backache. You may imagine all manner of illness—kidney infection, fibroid tumors, ovary problems—before you realize the obvious. A new mother spends much of her time carrying a 10- to 20-pound baby with one arm and a bag stuffed with bottles, baby food, diapers, clothing, and toys with the other. Breast-feeding in a strained position and bending and stooping to pick the baby up from a crib, a playpen, or the floor are activities certain to cause aches and pains in the neck, back, and legs.

"Lots of patients, new mothers included, often suspect serious illness rather than back pain. Kidney infection and cancer are the most common concerns," explained Jeffrey S.

Hansen, a chiropractor. The new mothers he treats typically experience low back pain from lifting and bending improperly, along with neck and shoulder pain from carrying heavy bags and poor posture while nursing or rocking their baby.

To help avoid lower back discomfort, Hansen said I should always bend my knees when picking a baby up off the floor or out of a playpen. The best way to lift a child is to squat down, gather the child to your body, then stand up. This prevents strain on the lower back, Hansen said, and is a great exercise for the legs. Also, he warned, never use one arm to lift a child off the floor.

"Put down the diaper bag or the bottle or whatever, and use both hands," Hansen advised.

Slumping forward while nursing a baby puts tremendous stress on the neck and upper back. Hansen said the ideal position for nursing is in a slightly reclined chair, so that the mother doesn't tilt her head too far forward. Most lactation nurses recommend placing a newborn on a pillow to raise the child up to the proper level for breast-feeding. As the child grows, you may have to move the pillow to the side so that it supports your elbow and let the baby lie in your lap.

Another hazard to a new mother's back is something we all do and will probably continue to do: carrying our child propped on our hip. The rule for carrying a heavy diaper bag on your shoulder applies here, and that is to switch sides often.

Hansen suggested new mothers gradually strengthen back muscles and increase flexibility with a regular program of stretches and exercises. As with all exercise programs, you should check with your doctor or chiropractor before you begin.

He recommended the following exercises for me:

Lie on the floor with your lower back flat and bring each knee to the chest for thirty seconds, then bring both knees to the chest for one minute. With feet downward and the lower back still flat on the floor, curl your upper body toward your pelvis, cup your hands over your kneecaps, and hold for two to three seconds.

Start on hands and knees and arch the back upward by bringing the pelvis forward and chin to chest while tightening abdominal muscles; hold for two to three seconds. Shift to a sitting-on-heels position with arms outstretched. Return to starting position, then shift back so you are sitting on right heel and stretch arms to the left. Repeat, shifting to the left heel with arms outstretched to the right.

Stand with your back to a wall and slowly turn your body (shoulders and hips) to place both hands on the wall behind you.

Standing facing a corner, place hands on opposite walls at shoulder level. Lean in toward the corner, keeping chest up and exhaling as you move.

Bend over a table, palms flat on surface, chin in, and arms straight. Raise upper back toward ceiling, inhaling. Exhale as you relax and lower your spine, pulling shoulder blades close together.

Weight loss if you are still over your prepregnancy weight and sleeping on a firm mattress with proper neck support will also you avoid the discomfort of back pain.

Month seven

A VIEW FROM DOWN UNDER

I never realized how easy I had it until Jesse began to crawl. For five months I could lay him on the floor in the middle of a soft, clean blanket surrounded by toys, and fully expect him to be there the next time I looked.

During the sixth month, he was creeping, but couldn't move fast enough to get out of the safe zone I had established in the middle of the family room.

At seven months, he was adept at rolling and wiggling across the floor but was not yet what I would define as mobile. He would get up on all fours, rock back and forth, gathering momentum, then pass gas and propel himself forward. Well, he didn't always pass gas while attempting to crawl, but it happened often enough to become a family joke. It must have been the strain of pulling his stomach up off the floor.

He experienced his first real bump on the head during

one of the gas-propelled lurches. Usually, he would make a head-first landing onto one of the many pillows I had surrounded him with, get up, and try it again.

This time, however, he overshot the pillow and made direct contact with the unpadded, wooden leg of the couch. It left a reddish mark, which later turned into a lumpy bruise right in the middle of his forehead. My first gut reaction was to get rid of all the furniture and decorate the house with bean bags.

As your baby's mobility increases, you will have to begin thinking about the visible dangers as well as the invisible ones. When Jesse began to crawl, so did I. Following the recommendation of more experienced moms, I dropped to my knees to get a better view of his world, looking for electrical cords and outlets at his level and for small objects he could easily choke on.

I was amazed at what I found down under my normal level of existence: lost pocket change, pens and pencils, fossilized popcorn and old, very old, chew toys discarded by the dog during puppyhood. I vacuum my floors every week, sometimes more often than that, but somehow these items had managed to hide under the couch, behind chair legs and in the folds of the curtains. Now seemed to be a good time for a professional carpet cleaning.

Identifying these obvious dangers was easy. What I didn't think about was something as seemingly harmless as grass or as invisible as pesticide residue. One beautiful, warm afternoon, I decided it would be fun to let Jesse crawl around in the front yard, experiencing the feel and smell of freshly mown summer grass.

Less than an hour later, angry red welts began to appear on the palms of his hands, on his wrists, and across his legs—everywhere the grass had touched. The pediatric nurse recommended I give him an over-the-counter liquid children's allergy medication containing diphenhydramine hydrochloride and apply an anti-itch lotion. It wasn't necessary to bring him into the office unless the rash spread or he developed signs of breathing difficulty, she said.

An allergy to grass, she said, is not uncommon in babies at this age. Generally, they grow out of it, and she recommended waiting a few months and trying again. She also questioned me about pesticides, and I later learned that my husband had sprayed the yard for ants the day before our little adventure. If pest control or herbicide products are used on the lawn, she advised waiting at least two days before putting the baby down to play there.

It is a dangerous world outside the womb. The best a mother can do is find a balance between protecting her baby from the hazards of life and allowing him to explore his new world with undaunted fearlessness.

It was during this precarious stage of Jesse's development that I began to have nightmares and dreadful waking fantasies involving potential dangers to my child. Frequently, while sitting in traffic, nursing, or as I drifted off to sleep at night, I would act out such a scene in my mind—an earthquake, a fire, a flood in which my child was endangered. Several nights in a row I dreamed that I forgot to take my child out of the car when I went shopping, only to return and find paramedics surrounding the vehicle. I was terrified that these dreams and waking fantasies revealed some unconscious resentment toward my baby.

According to Dr. Hickman (we spoke with her about postpartum depression in chapter 1), this is a common symptom of anxiety seen in many new first-time mothers. Like postpartum depression, it is also closely related to hormones and an increase in adrenaline.

"These nightmares and what we refer to as 'bad thoughts' can be frightening and intrusive for a new mother. They don't fit the way she sees herself as a loving mom," Dr. Hickman explained. "It is normal for all people to have bad thoughts, but we usually ignore them, dismiss them."

These imaginings of disaster are tools our mind uses to keep us vigilant and aware of the possibility of danger in our world. New mothers, Dr. Hickman said, may feel such high anxiety about the safety of their child that the thoughts "get stuck." This hypervigilance, she said, is seen as a defense mechanism. Some mothers even have fantasies about actually harming their child.

"These thoughts are nothing. They are not dangerous. When such thoughts become voices outside the head, then it is time to worry. Unfortunately, when a mother needs to be concerned about such thoughts, she may not be able to recognize there is a problem. Hopefully, others around her, her family, will see it and get help for her," Dr. Hickman continued.

Almost every night for a year, Kelli dreamed that her son was rolling off the bed and she couldn't catch him. "I would walk in my sleep and be up all during the night looking for him on the floor, under the bed. It was so weird because we never allowed Jordan to sleep in the bed with us, and we never left him lying on the bed unattended."

Her family had become very concerned over this recurring nightmare, and when Jordan was about a year old, Kelli discussed the problem with her doctor. "After I told a third person, someone outside the family, it just stopped."

Nightmares like these and waking fantasies like my own, Dr. Hickman reassured me, do not mean that we want something tragic to happen to our baby, that we don't love our child with all our heart. They are, she said, simply a harmless way of coming to terms with our fears and anxieties, a reminder of how fragile our children are and how vigilant we need to be.

From the Fast Track
to the Laugh Track

Not only do you have to worry about the dangers of your child's new mobility, you also have to fear profound embarrassment over the antics of a newly mobile little human. A crawling baby is a misadventure waiting to happen, and invariably it happens when everyone is watching.

Jennifer and John had taken their baby out to eat at a popular pizza restaurant at Newport Beach's exclusive Fashion Island shopping complex. Collin had one of those diaper disasters that oozed up the back and out the sides. A fresh diaper and a change of clothing was necessary. The bathroom did not have a changing table, and Jennifer was forced to lay Collin down on the floor. (Now you know why they put those changing pads in diaper bags.)

She managed to get him cleaned up and had turned away to get a clean outfit, when Collin rolled over, leaped to all fours, and, with the speed of an Olympic sprinter, crawled under the nearest occupied stall. Jennifer made a grab for him but missed.

"Under the door I could see red, spiked heels and pantyhose gathered around a woman's ankles—and my son pulling himself up on her knees," Jennifer recalled.

Moments later the woman emerged from the stall, dressed to the nines in a slinky dress and glittering jewels, holding Collin in front of her as if he were a bomb about to explode.

I guess that's one way to make new friends in strange places. Jennifer, however, said it was the most embarrassing moment of her life—until, that is, a few months later, when Collin, who had just discovered the fine art of spitting, sprayed mashed something or other into the face of a total stranger who had stopped by their table to admire "such a cute baby boy."

Jennifer said they don't eat out much anymore.

TOOLS OF THE TRADE

Mortifying baby antics are not the only thing a new mother must take in stride. Another is a plethora of baby paraphernalia. By the seventh month, my house was filled to overflowing with baby products, large and small. Like most upwardly mobile new moms, I had fallen prey to the lures of an array of baby catalogs that had suddenly begun to appear in my mailbox. How did they know this house now contained an uncertain new mother eager to buy whatever would make her baby healthier, happier, and more secure?

I used to get quite exasperated with my friends who had children. They couldn't go anywhere without all this baby stuff, and invariably, they left a trail of it behind them. Perhaps, like Hansel and Gretel, they just hoped to be able to find their way home again.

One friend would come to visit with her two (or was it three?) children once or twice a year. The house would look like an explosion at Toys 'R' Us. There would be dolls, games, books, food, diapers, and baby clothes covering every flat surface. And always, after they had gone home, I would find an assortment of left-behinds to box up and send along after them.

I still don't quite understand how this happens, but I do know that I have now joined the club. I've left behind bibs, bottles, and containers of food and juice at Grandma's house, at friend's homes, and even at restaurants and department stores. The only thing I haven't left—yet—is the baby.

ROLL OVER, ROVER

Something else that often gets left behind in the wake of a new baby is your pet. My dogs have always been my babies, relegated to virtual human status with their own beds and toys and kitchen privileges. But when we brought Jesse home from the hospital, our dog, Scout, instantly became just a dog.

Initially, I was very concerned that Scout would be jealous of the new member of our family. We were very careful to give him plenty of attention during that transitional time and to make sure he was properly introduced to the baby. We made sure he became accustomed to the sight, sound, and smell of his new human.

Later, after it was obvious that the dog had accepted Jesse into the family pack, my greatest concern was that Scout would inadvertently hurt the baby in an attempt to play with him, so we were very conscientious about never leaving them together unattended. Eventually, as Jesse became more mobile, the dog began to spend more and more time outside, because I could not keep the canine hairs off a baby who was rolling and crawling around on the carpet, and I couldn't keep their toys separated. Neither of them seemed to mind, but I had a hard time watching Scout chew on a teething ring while Jesse gnawed on an old rawhide bone. At best, I guess it taught them both the concept of sharing.

"The majority of the time, dogs and children become best of friends, but it can be worrisome at first—especially if it's an older dog that you've had for quite a long time," says David Thain, a Montana-based veterinarian.

"Often, dogs do become jealous and very aggressive when a baby is brought into the home," Thain says. "Major damage can be done very rapidly. Even a small dog, like a dachshund, can cause serious injury or death to an infant. A baby's pitched scream can send a dog into a frenzy."

Dogs that present a particular risk include those that have been purposefully taught to be aggressive. Additional training and socializing with other people and pets can help curb aggressive tendencies, Thain said. Sometimes neutering is recommended.

Thain said it is typical for pets to be ignored and pushed aside by their previously attentive owners when a new baby enters the picture. "You just don't have the time you once had to give to your dog, and this can result in behavior problems, like chewing on the furniture or having accidents in the house, to get your attention."

Even if the pet seems to easily accept your newborn, Thain said parents should watch for signs of a problem as the baby becomes more mobile. "An older baby who grabs at the dog, chews on its ears, and hits it can provoke an attack in a dog that has not previously shown any signs of aggression. The tantrums of the terrible twos can also prompt abnormal behavior in your pet."

An unusual submissiveness, such as "slinking around" can also be a warning.

"Things can happen so fast," Thain says. "If you have any concern about aggression, about the possibility of an attack, get rid of the dog. You can always find another dog, but you can't replace that child."

I still took care of our dog's physical needs in much the same manner that I always had, but sometime during the second half of my first year as a mother, it dawned on me that my attitude about our pet had changed drastically.

I have always been an animal lover and recall being surprised a few years ago when my friend Margaret, having stepped into the realm of motherhood, commented that she just didn't have much time for her once-beloved cat. I remember thinking that she must not love animals as much as I, or she would simply find the time and energy to give both to her new baby and her pet. Now that I'm a mother, I understand what she meant.

Anne, another dog fancier, was much the same way. Before she became a mother, her dog was her baby. The pup went everywhere with her. After her daughter was born, she said, "My dog is suddenly just a dog."

Kelli and her husband, a veterinarian, are avid animal lovers and have always treated their pets as part of the family. "I have always loved animals so much, and when I found out I was expecting, I guess I just thought the baby would be an extra special little animal to love. My mother kept telling me how different it would be, but I just couldn't comprehend until Jordan was born. I never knew I could love so much or worry so much."

Before we became mothers, our pets filled some maternal void. We may still care for our pets, but our baby's needs and our needs as a new mother must come first.

WHEN ONCE IS ENOUGH

At some point in their first year, many new mothers develop a fear, almost a paranoia, about becoming pregnant again.

For me, it happened at seven months. Other mothers I talked to experienced this anxiety around the end of the year.

This anxiety creates a multitude of conflicting emotions. When the thought first crossed my consciousness, I felt a fleeting whisper of elation. I had not really enjoyed pregnancy, and the first few months of motherhood were not exactly fraught with merriment. Yet the sweetness of holding my newborn was a taste I could gladly savor again.

But this was a brief sensation, quickly overshadowed by sheer terror. I was barely coping with raising one child. How could I possibly contemplate having two in diapers? I bought a home pregnancy test but was afraid to use it for two days. What a relief when the test was negative!

Many things—intestinal flu, indigestion, hormonal shifts due to breast-feeding or birth-control measures, fatigue—can mock the symptoms of pregnancy. Oral contraceptives and hormone injections used to make the ovaries "rest" can also cause weight gain, nausea, breast tenderness, and abdominal cramps.

If you are breast-feeding, you probably won't menstruate, so you won't have that monthly reassurance that you are not pregnant. A lot of women, especially young women with their first child, still believe (or at least want to believe) the old wives' tale that says you can't get pregnant as long as you are nursing a baby.

While nursing does delay a return of menstruation for many women, some nursing mothers do ovulate and can become pregnant before they even have had a period to warn them, my gynecologist explained. You can also verify that with my mother-in-law, who gave birth to seven children in less than fourteen years. And she breast-fed them all!

I had not planned my first pregnancy, but in the months of waiting for Jesse's birth, I came to believe God gave me a baby because he knew I needed one. It filled a hole in my heart left by my father's death a few months before and by the move to California a couple of years before that—a transfer that had uprooted me from my friends and family and from the South that I love so dearly.

I did not, however, need a second child at this juncture. My heart was full, and so were my hands. I just wasn't sure if God realized this.

In the days preceding my pregnancy panic, I had experienced some stomach problems, a little nausea, and was feeling more than normally fatigued. We were having an unusual heat spell—temperatures soaring above 100 degrees—which might have accounted for the unusual sleepiness and the nausea. I seemed to be urinating more often, too, but because of the heat, I was drinking more water.

I had logical explanations for all of my symptoms, yet I managed to convince myself that I was pregnant even though I had been using one of the most reliable birth-control methods available, an injection of synthetic hormone touted to be 99 percent effective.

Chalene experienced a similar panic attack when her son was about a year old. She had a flu, and the symptoms were very similar to what she had experienced during early stages of pregnancy.

"Sometimes I'm sad that he's not a baby anymore, but I don't want to have another one right now. It's just too taxing on me. I've seen too many women lose their minds with two in diapers," she said, relating the story of a friend with two small children.

"I admired her so much after she had her first baby," Chalene said. "She was so patient with her son. Now, she has a second baby, and the first is always in 'time out.'"

Lisa expressed similar sentiments: "I have a very, very

good child, very normal. I wouldn't take a million dollars for her, but I don't know if I could do it again."

But not all new mothers feel like this. As their babies approach toddlerhood, many mothers long for another infant to cuddle.

"I'd be pregnant already if we didn't have a big family vacation planned next summer," said Anne when her daughter, Tori, was 11 months old. "We had always planned on having a number of children while we are still young, but right after Tori was born, I told Wayne I wasn't sure I wanted any more children. I didn't know how I could possibly love another one so much, or give so much of myself."

A friend with five children explained it in a way Anne said she could relate to: "You love hamburgers and you love pizza and you love chicken. But they are all different, and you love them differently."

When Tori was only 6 months old, Anne held a friend's newborn baby and was surprised when she didn't feel even the slightest urge to have another baby. But when Tori was almost 11 months old, Anne held another friend's newborn and "felt it pull at my heart strings. At six months, I wasn't ready to even think about it, but at 11 months, I guess I was."

Every first-time mother, Anne said, must question whether or not she can commit herself as much to a second child as she did to her first. "I wonder if it will take a little bit away from what I feel for Tori. But at the same time, I want the excitement of being pregnant again. I can see Tori's own unique personality emerging, and I'm ready for the mystery of wondering what the next child will be like."

Month eight

LOOKING FOR MR. MOM

A new man emerged in the late eighties and early nineties. A "Mr. Mom" who shared equal responsibilities for raising the children. He changed diapers, mashed and strained homemade baby food, read the children to sleep at night and carried the baby for long walks in a daddy backpack. I don't know this man. Perhaps he's a myth, created by marketing departments so male models would look realistic while posing in catalogs that sell daddy-oriented baby paraphernalia.

My own partner has sort of eased himself gradually into fatherhood, as if he were stepping into a hot tub with the temperature set just a little too high. Whereas most mothers have to dive in headfirst, fathers generally can go a little more slowly. In the early months, he was eager to hold Jesse but just as eager to pass him over to Mom when he began to cry or needed a diaper change.

By our eighth month, he would volunteer to feed the

baby or watch him for an hour or two on the weekends while I went shopping. He was, of course, always ready to take part in playtime and had begun to help get Jesse to sleep in the evenings. But he had yet to change a diaper, give a bath, or dress a wiggling, recalcitrant child who has decided it's much more fun to leap from the changing table than to lie still as you struggle with a dozen tiny snaps and buttons.

Other mothers tell me I should insist that Daddy take a more active part in raising Baby, but I am still feeling a certain amount of pity for him following his first, rather traumatic experience of being left alone with his son. I suppose I owe him a little sympathy and understanding in light of how hard and how long I laughed at his dishevelment after only a half-hour alone with a hungry baby.

It had not been a particularly good day. I was up at 4:30 that morning to feed, bathe, and dress the baby and get myself ready to leave the house by 6:30 for a trip up the coast to Ventura. Our nephew was being confirmed, and it would be an all-day trip.

While it was good to be with family for such an important event, it was exhausting for me. I was up late the night before (it now takes two days to get ready for a one-day trip), and I was irritable from lack of sleep. Jesse was having one of his "hungry" days, and it seemed that I was constantly feeding him, removing a wet diaper, or changing his clothes after he'd soaked through them. I hadn't eaten all day, and by 3 P.M., when I finally got a chance to sit down and enjoy some of the wonderful food that had been prepared, it was time to pack up and leave.

On the return trip, we stopped at the hospital to visit Harold's father. We were a little paranoid about hospital germs and didn't want to take the baby inside. My mother-in-law and I went in first and left Harold with the baby, who was sleeping like a little angel in his car seat. Jesse was still breast-feeding, but I kept a bottle of "ready to feed" formula in the diaper bag for emergencies. I stayed about thirty minutes before returning to the car so my husband could go in to visit. We had parked at the far end of the lot, under the shade of a large tree.

As I approached, I could see Harold leave the car and start walking toward me, the baby squirming in his outstretched arms. I had never seen my husband look like he did at that moment: hair mussed (as if he had been raking his hands through it), clothes rumpled, tie hanging loose. There was a long, milky wet stain running down his shirtfront, under his arm and across the seat of his pants. His eyes were wide and a little glazed.

" 'Gitchy gitchy goo' didn't work. 'Booga booga boo' didn't work," Harold stammered as he thrust the baby into my arms.

My husband does not normally stammer.

"I tried to give him a bottle. He spit it up everywhere. Everywhere. Can you get this off of me? He wouldn't stop screaming the whole time you were gone. People kept staring. I thought I was going to be arrested for child abuse."

I guess I should be sorry my husband had to go through such an experience, but it did make me feel somewhat vindicated for the discomfort of pregnancy and the pain of labor.

And I liked that warm feeling I got when I looked down into the red, tearstained face of my son and was rewarded with a welcoming smile. There are times when only Mom will do.

Besides, I hadn't seen anything that funny in months—my husband, the tough guy, always in control of every situation, so obviously vanquished in a battle of wills with a tiny baby.

Despite this rather ignominious start, I didn't want

Harold to be just an observer in our son's first year. So many fathers wait until their children are a little older and easier to communicate with to begin taking an active part in their care.

But this is not always their fault or their choice. Many mothers, especially first-time mothers, say they find it difficult to let go of the controls long enough for their husbands to participate in raising Baby.

"I probably would have gotten more help from my husband when Alexis was a baby if I had not been Wonder Mother from the very beginning," said Lisa. "I thought I was supposed to do everything, and I shoved him out. So now he doesn't know what to do."

After talking to Lisa, I promised myself to let go a little more often and not step in and take charge whenever the baby got fussy or needed attention. Harold might not do it just the way I would, but that does not mean his way is not just as good.

If you have fallen into an unbreakable routine at home, where you are the sole child-care giver, it may help to change your environment—to get away for a few days and let a vacationing daddy take a more active part. When Jesse was 8 months old, we took a week-long trip to the hills and lakes of northern Arkansas. It seemed much easier to share child-care responsibilities with my husband while we were on the road than in our own home, where I have my routine.

It is important for a new mother to recognize that her husband has a new role to play as well and that his life has been changed just as drastically, although in different ways, by this all-consuming relationship with Baby. As Jesse approached his nine-month birthday, I was happy to find that we were sharing him and the responsibility of raising him much more equitably.

We're still, however, working on the diaper thing.

A TIMELY IDENTITY CRISIS

"Time," Harold said, when I asked him what he thought had changed the most about our relationship as a couple. "We never used to think about what time it was. If we wanted to do something, we just did it. If we wanted to go somewhere, we just went."

This once spontaneous lifestyle had become restricted by the need to time all of our activities around Jesse's eating and sleeping schedule. I could no longer just grab my purse and hit the road. I had to assemble a diaper bag suitable for whatever amount of time we would be gone from home, change the baby's clothes, and make sure he was fed and wouldn't get hungry before we got to wherever we were going. And then there's that diaper you have to change in the driveway because he had the "urge" just as you began to back out.

I realized that having a baby had irrevocably changed our lifestyle. This was inevitable. But I didn't realize how much it had changed our relationship until my husband also admitted that he didn't think of me as an individual anymore.

"Now, whenever I think about you, or speak about you to someone else, it's 'Susan and Jesse' instead of just 'Susan,'" Harold said.

I was having an identity crisis and hadn't even noticed. I wasn't really hurt by his observation. It was not said with malice but with a certain amount of surprise, as if he was unaware of his feelings until I posed the question. And it was easy to understand why he would feel this way. He rarely saw me without Jesse attached to some part of my body. When Harold left for work in the morning, I was usually nursing the baby, and when he returned in the evening,

I would again be nursing the baby. Or, if I was preparing dinner, Jesse would be on the kitchen floor, trying to pull up on my legs.

I realized then that if I wanted my husband to see me as he once had—even just a brief glimpse of the woman he fell in love with—I would need to act more like a mate and less like a mother when he was around. Dinner out, just the two of us, with some pasta, a bottle of wine, and maybe a strolling musician was definitely in order.

Our time alone together had become rare, usually restricted to brief periods while the baby napped. It would take a concerted effort to reestablish the couple part of our relationship.

Being a good mother was, is, and always will be a priority, but to be a good mother, a woman also must be a well-rounded individual with interests outside the realm of her family. You need to be able to talk to your husband about something other than what the baby did today.

Every new mom needs something that stimulates her having nothing to do with her baby or her husband. I made the affirmation to do something nice for myself at least once a week. Sometimes this means nothing more than curling up for an hour with a good book—a nice, juicy romance in which the heroine never changes a diaper or does the laundry.

"I really don't do many things that are just for myself," Anne said. "I'm very involved in my mom's group. I do mom's night out, but I do these things to make myself a better mother. When I work on my diet and exercise and other health issues, it's not for me as much as because I want to be here to take care of my family. Everything I take pleasure in now is connected with my family. Even when I buy clothes for myself, I'm thinking, 'Does Tori have something like this, so we can be coordinated?' "I take pride in not being just Anne anymore, but in being Tori's mom and Wayne's wife," she added.

Linda, however, said she has to "do something for myself." She rented space at a craft consignment shop and sells many of the items she makes at home—wreaths, candles, plaques, plates, and other decorative items. "I need to feel that I'm producing."

Kim said she still feels very much an individual, although she recognizes her own needs are rarely a priority now. "I have taken up golf. That's about the only thing I do for myself. And I go to the gym. I do that for myself and to get out of the house." She has also begun to write children's stories and poems in her "spare" time, not necessarily for publication but to satisfy her own sense of creativity and self-worth.

Many of the new mothers I have talked with say they haven't lost their identity as much as they have simply changed it, evolved into someone with a new, more focused interest. One thing they all agree on, however, is that their sensitivity to the world around them has changed.

CHANGING CHANNELS

I used to be able to watch violent movies and read Stephen King novels. Now, I have trouble watching the nightly news. Those emergency reenactment shows and medical dramas are definitely out. I can't even watch Arnold or Sylvester blast the bad guys without thinking, "That villain is somebody's baby." And that's fiction. Reality is even harder to take.

When so many children died or were injured in the bombing of the Oklahoma City federal building, I felt actual physical pain. I remember holding my baby almost constantly for two or three days following the tragedy, as I sat glued to the television screen.

Many mothers were surprised when I told them how much bad news now bothered me. "I thought it was just me. That I was the only one who felt like that," said Laura, whose son was born a few weeks after mine.

"Motherhood changes the way you react to everything," she continued. "I can't even stand to watch the news anymore, especially if it involves a child being hurt. I just cringe when I hear about anything like that. Maybe it's because we know how helpless and vulnerable they are, and we worry so much about our own."

Kelli also said she has become a much more fearful person since her son, Jordan, was born. "I used to be a brave person, but that is one way motherhood has changed me. Now I'm paranoid! I don't want to be like my grandmother—afraid of everything. But my attitude about everything has changed."

Even some of her favorite television shows are now off-limits. "I can't even watch *ER* anymore, especially if the show is about a kid being sick or hurt. I'm just so afraid of losing him."

This angst of motherhood, this trepidation that something or somebody will harm our child, changes a mother's view of the world. I worry more now about things that once seemed far removed from my tiny sphere of existence—the world economy, crime, disease, the environment, war, and everything else that might affect my son as he grows into adulthood. I feel proud when he achieves a new level of development—the first crawl forward, the first step. Yet these milestones also frighten me, because I know each step will take him farther from the realm of my protection.

Month nine

Is There an Echo in Here?

By the time Jesse was 9 months old, I was saying no so often the sound bounced off the walls continuously. Our dog was so confused, he just stayed outside, where he knew he wasn't in trouble.

You probably won't have much occasion to say no to your child or to reprimand him until the second half of his first year, when his mobility is increasing almost daily and his curiosity is unquenchable. It is a simple word, but it can be very difficult to say, especially for a mother who wants her baby to love her and doesn't want to make him cry.

The first time I said no to Jesse in a really stern tone of voice, his lower lip trembled, and he began to emit a terrified staccato wail punctuated by hiccuping sobs. My heart broke, and I spent the next ten minutes comforting and apologizing. His distress made me almost forget why I had said no in the first place—he was using my nipple as a teething ring.

By the seventh month, he could understand from the tone of my voice what I meant by no. His reaction to the command ranged from shattered outrage and frustration to quiet consideration. By nine months, he had learned to expect a no to follow certain actions, like pulling the lamp off the end table by its cord or banging on the television screen with his favorite toy car. He would reach for the lamp cord, then look to see if I was watching before proceeding with his plan of action. If I said no or shook my head, he would pause, hand in midair, and think about it before continuing or deciding to go on to something else.

If you haven't done it already, nine months is a good time to babyproof your home to whatever degree works best for you and your family. That may mean removing virtually everything that can be broken, shredded, ripped apart, or eaten, including the family pet. Or it may mean taking only a few major safety precautions—installing gates at the top and bottom of stairways, for instance, or locking cabinets that contain harmful chemicals.

I asked myself what I wanted—a bare coffee table, stripped of all our adult treasures, and a child free to explore, or an immaculate, picture-perfect home filled with the echo of a thousand nos bouncing off the walls.

At first I did not plan to remove the treasures from his reach. After all, my mother said she never put anything away when my brother and I were small. I thought I could exhibit the same diligence, but gradually, I found myself removing, or simply moving to increasingly higher levels, many of the objects I didn't want Jesse to get his hands (and mouth) on.

"I just put everything away for a while and took it back out after his first birthday," said Marcia. "And he spent a lot of time in a playpen."

When Jesse was born, friends presented us with a new playpen as a shower gift. I looked upon it with some misgivings. I didn't want to restrict his exploration by keeping him in a playpen or a swing all the time. I wanted to encourage his curiosity and adventurous spirit. That is a wonderful sentiment for a brand-new mom to express. What I didn't know, novice that I was, is how impossible it is to constantly watch a 9-month-old who seems to be able to crawl faster than you can walk.

No matter how much you put away, you can't babyproof your home completely. When you find yourself constantly putting things away and shouting no in unison with your spouse every thirty seconds, it is time to put your heads together and develop a singular style of discipline. The first step is to agree on where the boundaries are, what things you will allow your little explorer to investigate unhampered, and what things he is not allowed to touch.

"Your job as a parent is like a greenhouse to a seedling," said Karan Sims, a certified instructor and trainer for the International Network for Children and Families. "You have to filter out most of the harmful experiences, but let enough of them in so he can experience life."

Sims teaches parenting classes and gives talks to new mothers on how to discipline without resorting to corporal punishment and how to raise a baby without saying no all the time.

"You have to learn how to be firm and kind at the same time. Most of us don't have role models for that. We grew up in households where one parent was autocratic and the other was jelly," Sims told a group of parents and expectant parents at a YWCA class.

"Our parents expected their kids to be obedient. Period. That didn't work for the next generation, and society became too lenient with kids. We don't have any role models for middle of the road," she said.

What works best in today's society, is a "reasonable" approach. You should reason with your child and give him choices and alternatives to bad behavior.

"It's never too young to start. At nine months, he may be too young to fully understand, but it sets a pattern of behavior," Sims said. "They are in a learning stage. How we act and react determines how they learn from their own mistakes."

At nine months, children begin to assert themselves in sometimes unpleasant ways. They are not misbehaving, Sims explained, but attempting to communicate with you in a more aggressive manner.

"From six months up until nine months, he was just a ball of fun," Chalene said of her son, Skyler. "But at nine months, he started throwing fits. He didn't want to be dressed; he didn't want his diaper changed. Everything was a big fight. I love my son, but at this stage I wasn't sure I liked him."

Jesse was also about 9 months old when he began to struggle through diaper changes. Instead of getting angry and yelling or physically restraining him through the ordeal, I tried offering him two toys to choose between before I began diapering. This seemed to distract him long enough to get the job done. Singing, whistling, and making animal sounds also helped. If anyone happened to walk by the window above the changing table at this time, the passerby would undoubtedly think I had lost my mind.

When it comes to establishing bedtimes and meal schedules, Sims recommended parents "take your cues from your children, but don't let them run amok. You set the parameters."

"When our kids are little, we are so busy, so concerned

with how to make them eat their peas and go to bed at night, that we don't see the big picture," she continued. "What kind of characteristics do you want your child to have as an adult, and how do you encourage those traits?"

The qualities you admire most in an adult—assertiveness, self-confidence, an eagerness to learn—are sometimes the things that drive you crazy as the parent of a newly toddling baby.

"Don't get hung up on the small potatoes—or the peas. Think about your child's happiness and self-esteem and what they are learning from you. The family is like a microcosm of the world for your child, their view of life. They learn how to be a parent and a spouse from watching you."

Sims stressed building self-esteem from infancy on through childhood. "Stop focusing on their mistakes. Don't teach them to lie or cover up a mistake because they expect you to get angry and spew at them. Teach them to fix it."

Sims also recommends what she calls "the genuine encounter." When your child wants your attention, don't shut him out, she said. "Give him twenty seconds of direct eye contact. Focus on him with 100 percent of your being, even if it is only for a few seconds." This actually takes less time, she said, than a string of nos and certainly causes everyone less stress than spanking a child because he became frustrated by your indifference and misbehaved.

The genuine encounter works at any age. Even a crawling baby can tell the difference between a few moments of undivided attention and the rejection of being pushed aside until Mommy has more time.

It is also important, she said, to make sure your child knows he is loved, even if his actions are not. Whenever I say no to Jesse I wait until he has stopped whatever action prompted my command, then I give him a big smile. This usually prevents the tears that were about to fall because his wishes were thwarted.

I enjoyed the parenting workshop, and I liked the instructor's ideas on building self-esteem, but I knew it wouldn't always be as simple as she made it sound. One of the toughest challenges would be reaching a consensus with my husband over the punishments and incentives we would use to teach our child the values, morals, and behaviors we espouse.

I can see already that there are some things which will be acceptable to me but not to Harold and vice versa. For instance, it's not OK with me for the baby to French kiss the dog, but it doesn't seem to bother my husband. And though it bothers Harold for the baby to take a magazine from the coffee table and rip it to shreds, I will give Jesse an entire stack of periodicals if it keeps him quiet while I fix dinner.

As parents, we will undoubtedly disagree on discipline from time to time throughout Jesse's childhood. We have different assumptions about child rearing because we were raised in different households. That doesn't make either one of us right or wrong. Just different.

Harold was reared in a home where the rod (or the wooden spoon) was not spared whenever he or one of his six siblings stepped too far out of line. I can remember only two or three spankings in my entire childhood—once for doing something my mother had warned me was dangerous and another time for dropping matches on the carpet to see how long they would burn.

Sometimes I am not sure how to handle certain situations, but other times I make a quick decision based on mother's instinct, only to discover later that Harold has a completely different theory. For instance, I began buying safety products as soon as Jesse began to crawl—protectors for electrical outlets and gates to keep him away from the stairs. I was surprised when Harold said he wasn't sure we should install some of these devices. His theory was in two parts: A child needs to be taught no rather than be removed from things you don't want him to touch; and a child must fall down and get hurt a few times in order to learn what his limits are.

That's a pretty tough theory for a mother to follow. My instinct commands me to protect him from both falls and failures, but I know I must resist the urge to help him too often. His frustration when he fails at a task, such as reaching for a toy or pulling up on the coffee table, will only serve to make him work harder at achieving mobility, as well as other goals later in life.

However, my own nerves will remain much less frayed if I know he cannot fall down the stairs or electrocute himself. So, for my own sake, I installed a few safety devices.

Sometime during the first year parents should discuss their views and strike a compromise on the discipline issue somewhere between autocracy and jelly. One of the things Harold and I quickly agreed on was the need to be consistent and to follow through. If it isn't OK to play with the remote control today, then it shouldn't be OK to play with it tomorrow. When Jesse pulls on the lamp cord and I tell him no, I must follow through by making sure he stops. It's important, Harold and I decided, that he learn as early as possible that *no* does not ever mean *maybe*.

There are a great many theories out there on discipline. Everyone has an opinion, and like all advice, it must be taken with a grain of salt and applied to your own family situation.

FLEAS IN THE EAR

The old folks back home used to call unsolicited advice a "flea in the ear." Everyone who has ever raised a child (and some who haven't) becomes an expert on child rearing, and this free advice can be about as irritating as a bug in a body part to a new mom who is already under tremendous pressure to make endless decisions for her baby.

New mothers expect to get a lot of advice during the first few weeks after bringing Baby home from the hospital. I guess we all must learn to take this in stride, because it doesn't lessen with time. There is no shortage of advice out there, and you will get a steady flow of it from family members, friends, neighbors, baby-sitters, and even total strangers in waiting rooms, airport lobbies, and the grocery checkout line.

One first-time mother, who asked to remain anonymous for obvious reasons, said, "My mother-in-law asked if I minded if she gave me some advice. I wanted to say, 'As long as you don't mind if I don't take it,' but I just smiled and said, 'Not at all.'"

It was a little easier, but not much, for this same new mom to take her own mother's advice.

As a new mother, you will have a lot of questions for which there are no right or wrong answers. What works for your sister-in-law might not work for you, but that doesn't mean the advice should be ignored. You can learn a lot from the experience of others, but you have to trust your own instincts when it comes to deciding what is best for you and your baby.

If your baby has the hiccups and your mother suggests a bottle of sugar water, weigh that advice against your pediatrician's warnings about adding sugar or salt to your infant's diet. One friend may encourage you to begin feeding your baby cereal at four weeks, while another tells you this will do irreparable damage to your little one's digestive system.

Feeding, by breast or bottle, is one of the areas in which you can expect to get a lot of advice from all directions. Everyone, it seems, has an opinion—sometimes a rather strong one—on feeding choices, solid foods, and weaning.

Many babies exhibit a lessening of interest in breast-feeding around nine months, which makes it a good time to begin thinking about weaning and preparing for the switch to a bottle or cup. There have been many times during the year when I looked forward to the day my baby was fully weaned. But as he began to eat more solid foods and his nursings gradually dropped from six to five and then, suddenly, to four, I felt a twinge of nostalgia. I knew that my life (and my wardrobe) would be simplified, but I also knew that a part of me would truly miss breast-feeding.

One Lump or Two?

If I had found a lump in my breast a year or so ago, I would have been terrified. When it happened around Jesse's 9-month birthday, I knew that it was probably related to breast-feeding. Breast lumps in nursing mothers are usually the result of a clogged milk duct. The lump, though red and tender, is not serious in itself. If ignored and neglected, however, it can lead to infection and mastitis, an inflammation of the breast.

I thought I was being very conscious of and in tune with my body during this first year of motherhood. After all, a mother's body, especially if she is breast-feeding, is a crucial element in the physical and emotional health and well-being of her child. I was mindful of the need to eat a healthy, well-balanced diet and get plenty of sleep—and consummately guilty whenever I didn't do either.

But this was a very hectic time—I had work to complete and a vacation to plan—and I basically ignored a lump in one breast until it became a full-blown case of mastitis that required oral antibiotics to remedy.

A number of factors can contribute to a clogged milk duct. Nursing in one position, a bra that fits too tightly in one area, and skipping a feeding can all cause a milk duct to become plugged. A plugged duct is characterized by a tender lump that is hard and warm. It may even be a little red.

Typically this happens in the first four to six weeks of nursing, but it can occur at any time during breast-feeding, such as when Baby first begins to sleep through the night, and your breasts, used to several night feedings, become painfully engorged during those first few nights of uninterrupted slumber. When this happened to me around the fifth month, I used a small electric pump before bedtime to ensure my breasts were thoroughly emptied. After a few days, my body adjusted to the new schedule.

But at nine months, I had become such a pro at nursing that I did not take the same precautions I had in those earlier, novice months. Over time I had stopped worrying about keeping track of which breast I used last, and I based my decision on which one felt fuller. In the early months, I kept a safety pin on my bra so I would know where to start the next time. I had absolutely no short-term memory in those days.

In the ninth month, our nursing schedule dropped from five to four times a day—roughly 7 A.M., 11 A.M., 4 P.M., and 9 P.M. Also, Jesse was not nursing as long each time as he had before—maybe only once each day would he suckle for twenty minutes or more. It probably would have been wise on my part to use only one breast at each feeding during this transitional time to ensure that both were being emptied properly or to pump at least once a day, but I was preoccupied with life's little daily crises and unmindful of the potential for problems.

The first warning sign I paid attention to was a shooting pain that awakened me from a deep sleep during the early morning hours. The pain was so sudden and so intense that I immediately looked at my husband to see if he had grabbed me in his sleep, but he was sprawled innocently on his own side of the bed. I even nudged him a time or two just to make sure he wasn't faking those snores.

As soon as I realized I had a real problem, I tried the usual remedies: a five-minute application of a wet hot pack or a heating pad to soften the lump; varying the positions used for breast-feeding; offering the affected breast first; increasing the number of nursings as much as possible; and massaging the sore duct during feeding.

I also put away the new nursing bras I has just purchased. These were actually pretty, with some lace, a little bow, and an uplifting underwire. The latter may have been a contributing factor. If a bra is tight enough to leave an indentation in your skin, it might also be inhibiting milk flow and duct drainage, lactation specialists warned me.

If you follow these remedial procedures, a clogged duct will usually right itself within a day or two. If the condition persists or worsens, it may be an indication of mastitis, and you should contact your doctor.

After a couple of days of self-help that came too late, my lump had become a hot spot accompanied by red streaks on the underside of the breast. I was fatigued and running a slight fever, sure signs that the complaint had progressed into mastitis. In most cases, mastitis is caused by a bacterial infection, and the symptoms can be very similar to a flu—fever, chills, nausea, and muscle aches, as well as hot spots and pain in the affected area.

Mastitis, my doctor explained, is usually caused by the entry of germs from the baby's mouth into a milk duct. Although having dry, cracked nipples often facilitates the bacteria's entry into a milk duct, mastitis can occur even when this condition is not present.

In my own case, the doctor speculated, engorgement and plugged ducts were more than likely a contributing factor because we had begun the weaning process.

"Bacteria in itself won't hurt, but if it stays there in ducts that have not been emptied, it can create a problem," Dr. Blase said.

When I realized my own measures were not improving the situation, I called my doctor and described the symptoms, and she immediately prescribed an oral antibiotic. Within a few hours of my taking the first pill, the pain had lessened considerably, and after a week of medicine, the problem was resolved, with the only side effect being a new self-awareness and sense of caution on my part.

Of course, by the time I was over the mastitis, I had developed a yeast infection from taking the antibiotics. These are the times when a sex change sounds tempting. Do men realize how easy they have it? I've got to make sure my husband is aware of his blessings.

Month ten

Kodak Moments

The last three months of your child's first year are a time for mothers to savor. You have been told to do just that all year long, but were probably too tired and too busy to pay much attention to the advice.

By the tenth month, your child has fallen madly in love with you, and it is an unconditional love. He doesn't care if your hair isn't brushed, dinner isn't ready, and the laundry isn't done. You are the center of his universe and his window on the world.

Enjoy the moment. Don't let it pass unnoticed or unrecorded. Before you know it, he will be a terrible 2-year-old and will have learned to scream the word *no* over and over and over again. Then, suddenly, almost overnight, he will be sixteen, and you will be on *Oprah* discussing his weird wardrobe, indecipherable slang language, and proclivity for piercing body parts.

"The tenth month was just so much fun for me. You can actually see your baby learn things at this age," said Anne. "For instance, the telephone will ring and she will automatically say "Dada" because it's usually her daddy calling. And in the afternoon, she crawls to the door and says "Dada" because she knows it's time for Wayne to come home."

There are many things you will expect your 10-month-old baby to do—dance in front of the television screen when *Sesame Street* is on, imitate your gestures and facial expressions, play patty cake or peekaboo. Every child does these things. They are not unique. "But when it is your baby doing it, it is just so much cuter than when anybody else's baby does it," said Anne.

Jesse was almost 10 months old when he first initiated a game of peekaboo. I had been playing peekaboo with him for months, and he always seemed to enjoy it, but he had never started the game himself. Then, one Sunday afternoon, we were enjoying a rare lazy day together. Harold and I were watching television, and Jesse was playing on the floor at our feet, when I noticed him covering his eyes with a blanket and then peering over the top at me. I got so excited I called everyone I knew to spread the word. We had a child genius—he could play peekaboo!

A 10-month-old child is making so many steps forward that it is hard for most mothers, especially first-time mothers, not to bore friends and relatives with stories of their baby's wondrous new achievements. Perhaps that's why we often seek out other new parents. They understand our obsession and will pretend to listen politely, waiting patiently for us to shut up so they can talk about their own baby.

If you haven't already become an irrepressible shutter-bug (or if your compulsion to photograph your child on a daily basis dimmed after the first few awestruck months when every new expression demands to be recorded for posterity), now is the time to dust off the camera. I have several "good" cameras that I have used for professional newspaper and magazine work in the past, but I found my best shots during this stage of Jesse's growth were from the automatic "point and shoot" that I kept in his diaper bag. It was always ready for those fleeting moments that would have been missed in the time it takes to change a lens, attach a flash, and focus a more advanced camera.

You don't have to be a professional photographer to get great candid snapshots of your baby. Stuart Holt, an Arkansas photographer specializing in children's portraits, offered several suggestions for taking perfect pictures at home and for having successful (not stressful) studio photographs taken by a professional.

"The most important thing is to plan to do it when your baby is the happiest, and that differs with each child. It might be right after a nap, after a meal, or after a bath," Holt said.

"Second, don't plan or expect too much with little babies. The only thing you can depend on is that they are undependable," he continued. "You have a narrow window of opportunity with most babies. They have a very short attention span. If you don't get the picture you want in the first couple of shots, you may not get it that time."

Babies, he added, will let you know when they have grown tired of the photography game. "When they hit the wall, they'll let you know, and there is no point in going on. They will just get more and more frustrated, and you'll end up with red eyes and tearstained cheeks."

Bright colors, he said, usually make the best pictures, but babies, just like adults, have certain colors that compliment their eye and hair color (if they have hair) and skin tone.

"You don't want colors that detract from the baby. A lot of people still like pink and blue. The background should depend on the color and style of clothing. My personal favorite is white. Everything goes with it—even white," Holt continued.

There are several other steps you can take to ensure having a successful portrait sitting in a professional photography studio.

"Don't plan on too many outfit changes. It will just make them cranky. Make the clothes comfortable. Christening gowns with starched, frilly collars are uncomfortable, and the babies in them will get cranky in a hurry," Holt said.

If you want to capture a special smile or certain expression, like that adorable wrinkled-up nose, make sure you tell the photographer to use the right words or cues to elicit the desired look.

"Some kids I have told to smile and they either close their eyes or look like they are going to bite me," Holt said. "And don't be intimidated. Do whatever it takes to get your baby to smile. Act silly; make a funny face or weird noise. There was a lady in the studio today who was jumping up and down and flipping her ponytail over her head just to get her son to laugh."

No matter what you do, no matter how carefully you plan the photo session, getting that perfect shot is often just a matter of luck. "Sometimes you just stumble on it."

Holt recalled the mother who brought her baby girl into the studio for a beauty-pageant photograph. "We got two shots before she started to fuss and cry. But one of them was perfect, and she won the photogenic category in the pageant."

When selecting a studio, Holt said, make sure the photographer is experienced at taking baby portraits. "They might have years of experience as a photographer, but if they haven't worked with babies, you might have some problems. Also, be aware of any preferences or fears your child might have regarding a male or female photographer. Some babies are frightened by beards, for instance, and some work better with women."

Whether you are taking photographs at home or in a professional studio, Holt said, the key ingredient is a good sense of humor.

"Everybody has got to be comfortable," he said.

A few of the special "first" moments you will want to capture on film during the year will include the first bath, first taste of solid food, first haircut, the first crawl, and, of course, the first birthday party.

THROUGH THE EYES OF INNOCENCE

One of my favorite places to take candid photographs of Jesse was in our own front yard, where I could catch the look of wonderment on his face each time he made a new discovery.

It had been a very long time since I had been excited by the flight of a butterfly or intrigued by the industrious movement of an ant colony.

As Jesse began to cruise, his interest in the world outside our four walls grew with intensity. I could no longer leave the door open to an afternoon breeze without being prepared to pursue him into the great wilderness of our front yard.

I tried to imagine how immense and strange and wonderful it must all seem to him—towering trees, brightly colored hibiscus blooms, sweetly smelling gardenia blossoms, buzzing bees, and the hum of the big yellow truck churning cement for our neighbor's new driveway.

This is the best part of motherhood—being able to show your child the world and see it anew through his eyes. And there's no charge for admission.

I can't wait to show him clouds.

ONLY YOU

As your baby becomes more independent and more mobile, as his world expands beyond the confines of a few rooms, he may, conversely, become more and more dependent on you. He may be almost frantic in his need to be near you at times, typically, at the most inconvenient times. Pediatricians and other baby experts refer to this distress as "separation anxiety," but I came to think of it as the "kangaroo" syndrome because Jesse acted as if he wanted to climb into my pocket for the duration of childhood.

As long as I was within touching distance, he was content, sometimes seemingly oblivious to my presence. I could sit on the couch above him for half an hour without being noticed, but the minute I got up to leave the room, he would start to cry, the pitiful wail of one left abandoned and alone.

"This is typical," Dr. Ponzio said when I questioned her about Jesse's sudden attachment to me. "Usually it occurs between the ninth and tenth month. It is a developmental thing. Their understanding has developed to the point where they can recognize that you are leaving and they don't understand that you will come back."

As Jesse grew more aware of himself and his surroundings, he seemed to seek my attention, my companionship, and my approval on an almost constant basis. He wanted to do things for himself, but he needed me ever at his side. At eight months, he would play by himself for long periods of time while I worked nearby, maybe in the kitchen fifteen or twenty feet away. But at ten months, he would fret if I was more than a couple of feet from him, crawling after me, clinging to my legs, and pulling up on my shorts in an effort to get me to pick him up.

It was this little habit that led to one of my own most embarrassing moments of motherhood. I was just outside the front door, pruning a plant in a hanging basket. Jesse was crawling around at my feet, whining. I was determined not to give in and pick him up. I was not going to be one of those mothers who constantly carry a child around on their hip.

I guess he decided to take matters into his own hands. He stood up, grabbed the hem of my shorts, and tried to climb up the backs of my legs. Naturally, he lost his balance and fell down, taking the shorts with him. Naturally. And, of course, it was late afternoon and most of my neighbors were out in their yards, watering, pruning, laughing. I'm still not sure what I learned from this particular lesson of motherhood: to pick him up whenever he wants, to confine him to the playpen when I do yard work, or to invest in a good pair of suspenders.

In time I did learn how to avoid being manipulated by every whimper to be picked up and held, yet give him enough attention to keep him reasonably content while I went about my business. It worked some of the time. I also learned how to tell when he really needed comforting and I should forgo whatever task I was working at and just cuddle him for a while.

And I learned not to turn my back on him while wearing loose clothing.

If you can endure this stage with a sense of humor, compassion, patience, and stoic resolve, it will pass with much less trauma for both of you. More experienced moms advised me not to attempt to sneak away from Jesse when I left him with a sitter, as this would only create more anxiety for him. Making a ritual out of saying "bye-bye" and explaining to him that I would be back also seemed to help. He may not have been able to understand what I was saying, but my words were soothing. On a few occasions, I thought I would need a crowbar to pry Jesse loose from my legs as I headed out the door. With experience I learned this scene could be avoided if the baby-sitter distracted him with a toy, a game, or food.

"They do outgrow this separation-anxiety stage, but it may be a while," Dr. Ponzio said. "When he is old enough to get too busy, too involved in playing, then you will no longer be the center of his attention, and he will not mind quite as much when you leave."

I guess that's both the good news and the bad news. You don't want to be smothered by your baby, but it is kind of nice to be the center of someone's attention.

Along with being unusually clingy to his mother, a 10-month-old baby also may be a little more hesitant about strangers, new experiences, and unfamiliar objects than he was only a month prior. This is referred to as "stranger anxiety" and can begin at any point during the first year, although the eighth, ninth, and tenth months are typical for the onset.

These new anxieties on your child's part can be very disconcerting at times. The best cure is to take him with you to as many places as possible so he will become used to new experiences and unfamiliar places. Just try not to be too embarrassed when he screams in terror because the sales clerk smiled at him. I cut several shopping excursions short because I was afraid someone would assume I was beating my child and call the police.

In the first six months, most babies will bask in the attention of almost any adult. When Jesse was 5 and 6 months old, I was amazed and a little troubled that he would go so easily and quickly to anyone who held out his arms to him and cooed. I wondered if I would have to put a leash on him whenever we went out, just to ensure he didn't toddle off with a total stranger.

I needn't have worried. At 8, 9, and 10 months, he would cry, a frightened sob, arms reaching pitifully for me, whenever an unfamiliar person got too close. The stranger didn't even have to look at him. A store crowded with other shoppers busily going about their business could send him into a panic. This phase lasted only a few months, ending during the tenth month almost as abruptly as it had begun. His distress at being separated from me, however, stayed with him to some degree for the rest of the year.

Since Jesse's anxieties began about the time I started to use a baby-sitter on a more regular basis, I speculated that it might have been triggered by his realization that Mommy might be leaving him with the person attempting to pick him up. But our pediatrician said this is a normal stage of development that rarely has anything to do with what the parents do or don't do.

Many children experience both separation and stranger anxiety during the last few months of the first year. It is easy for a mother to become very frustrated by a clinging baby who crawls behind her, crying, each time she walks a few feet away and screams whenever anyone else tries to hold him. It is especially frustrating if he is his most demanding during dinner preparations or when you are trying to get ready to go out for the evening. (Some mothers actually do go out for the evening, or so I've heard.)

I tried to be sensitive to Jesse's fears and understand that he was still too young to grasp the concept that objects and people do not cease to exist just because they are out of sight. We played a game almost every day that I hope helped ease him through this anxious stage. I would get his attention with a favorite toy, hide the toy for a few moments, then bring it back into his vision. In time he seemed to be able to understand that, just like the toy, Mommy could leave and not be gone forever.

Ten months also is a time when many babies exhibit a preference for one parent over another, generally the mother if she is the primary care giver. This is a phase that can be very difficult for both parents to deal with and may leave one of them feeling slighted and left out. Most parents say it will pass in time, especially if the attitude is not reinforced either positively or negatively.

Stacey's daughter, Elizabeth, was about 10 months old when she entered this phase. "If I was there, she wouldn't go to anybody else. Sometimes not even her dad. I would hand her over to him so I could go to the bathroom, and she'd throw a fit," Stacey recalled.

"You can't reason with them when they are 10 or 11 months old. If it was not an emergency, I'd just take her," Stacey said. "I'm not going to force her to go to somebody else." Her husband, she said, "never took it personally. He was just relieved when I'd take her and she'd stop crying."

Most of the time, my son's absolute love for me brings me nothing but joy. There are days, however, when I feel a little smothered by his constant dependence on me. I keep reminding myself that someday I'll just be glad to get him to stay in the same room with me for more than a few minutes.

SOMETHING TO SINK YOUR TEETH INTO

At some point during the first year, most mothers must deal with the issue of teething. It can be inconsequential or it can be absolute hell, depending on which mother you talk with. Many babies begin getting their first teeth at around six or seven months, while some show no signs of teething until after their first birthday.

Jesse began to drool (copious amounts, I might add) during his fifth month, but he was 7 months old before the first incisors popped through the gums. By his tenth month, he had four top incisors and two bottom ones.

I had heard hair-raising horror stories from other moms about their children's distress during teething, but none of this occurred with Jesse. Minor discomfort and mild fretfulness were his only symptoms, along with, of course, buckets of drool and occasional ear tugging.

"Ear pulling is very common during teething," Dr. Ponzio explained. "Jaw pain is not localized. Even redness of the ears is not uncommon. There seems to be some connection between teething pain and the nerves and blood vessels in the ears."

Even though both my mother and my baby-sitter suspected an ear infection every time they saw Jesse tug at his ear lobes, Dr. Ponzio said not to be concerned unless he was also running a fever and had previously experienced some upper respiratory congestion. Apparent ear pain or a foul odor or discharge from the ear would be other signs that the problem was more serious than teething.

"An ear infection is more likely to follow a cold or flu," Dr. Ponzio said. "If he is pulling on his ear under those circumstances, then it might be an infection, and you should bring him into the office."

Now that Jesse had teeth and was beginning to use them for something other than gnawing on the coffee table, I wondered what I was supposed to do with them—ignore them because they will eventually go away, or rush out and buy a tiny electric brush?

Our family dentist suggested these first teeth be wiped with a clean, damp gauze pad or with a specially sized infant toothbrush. The dental hygienist suggested I try a soft rubber brush that fits over my own finger and is more easily maneuvered.

"Whatever you can do at this point is good. He's not going to let you mess around in his mouth for more than a few seconds without a struggle, so you don't need to worry about technique," she said. "But if he's eating solid foods and drinking sugary juices, you need to be cleaning his teeth daily."

The dentist also said toothpaste wasn't necessary although a very small amount could be used to flavor the brush, making it a little more interesting for baby. There would be no need to visit the dentist's office for a professional cleaning, she said, until Jesse was about 2½ to 3 years old, "unless he falls, which is common for toddlers, and breaks a tooth or injures his mouth." The first visit, she said, would probably not entail a cleaning, but would just be to "let him get used to the idea."

TRY THE BUFFET

Feeding your baby will still be consuming a major portion of your day (and most of your energy) in the tenth month. I wish I could tell you what to expect. It always seemed to help me if I could be prepared mentally, physically, and emotionally for my baby's next stage.

Unfortunately, about the only thing that is predictable about a 10-month-old baby's eating habits is that what goes in one end will inevitably come out the other.

The tenth month is a good time to introduce table foods, if you haven't done that already. Jesse had been sampling some of our own "adult" food for months. Everything from green beans to cheese pizza went down easily if cut into small enough pieces. As he entered the tenth month, I began to substitute tiny pieces of meat and cheese for spoonfuls of pureed baby food. Whole-wheat toast cut into small pieces and spread with creamy peanut butter was a suggestion from our pediatrician that was received with definite approval.

Some babies develop tremendous appetites toward the end of the first year, while others become finicky eaters, refusing to eat one day but eating everything in sight, even vegetables, the next day.

"It's hard to get Collin to eat good food. He prefers french fries. But the doctor said his weight is good, so I shouldn't worry so much about it," Jennifer said.

Many mothers struggle with this, turning meals into a battle of wills, leaving themselves and their babies in a state of frustration. It was almost impossible for me to resist the urge to coerce Jesse into taking "just one more bite" until he had cleaned his plate. But I know that forcing yourself (or your baby) to eat beyond the point of being full is not a good habit to develop, so I try to curb this compulsion on my part.

It is a hard fact to accept, but most babies know how much food they need. But that doesn't mean that your baby should be allowed to substitute junk—cookies or crackers—for quality food. This is especially easy to do when you are away from home, perhaps eating out in a restaurant, and you just want him to "be good" for a little while. From experience, I've learned you'll pay for this later, when he refuses to eat the "real" food you serve him when you get home.

I found whole-grain cereals to be a better choice than cookies and crackers when eating out, and the effort it took to grasp them and get them into his own mouth would keep him distracted for most of the meal. By the time he was 9 months old, I found that I could give him samples of most of the food on my own plate. The novelty of a new taste and texture would keep him relatively content while I enjoyed my meal, too.

Many of our friends had warned us that the tenth month would mark a dramatic change in our mealtime habits. Overnight, many mothers said, their children developed culinary independence and refused to take any food proffered by spoon. They wanted to feed themselves, and only finger foods and chunks that could be mashed, smeared, and volleyed into the next room were acceptable.

Now is a good time to invest in a vinyl mat to spread under the high chair. These decorated mats can be found for around ten dollars at department stores, toy stores, and in specialty catalogs. Old sheets and newspapers may not look as chic but work just as well for catching crumbs and splatters. Wipe-clean bibs with pockets to catch some of the overflow are a must, along with bowls that attach to the table or tray with suction.

Or you could just buy a dog. It didn't take our canine very long to figure out that there were tasty treats to be found in baby's wake. Whenever I let Scout into the house, his first priority is to scour the family room for fallen crumbs.

I knew that mealtime mess was just part of the learning experience and a good way for babies to find out about colors and textures, as well as cause and effect (squeeze a cracker and it will crumble) and gravity (a fistful of mashed squash will almost always fall to the floor when flung from tiny fingers). I knew that squash on the carpet and carrots on the wall were just a part of motherhood. The realization didn't make it any easier to watch, however.

CHEERS FOR THE TWO-FISTED DRINKER

Drinking from a cup is another major step in a child's development from a baby into a toddler, but making the decision to wean, either from the breast or a bottle, is never an easy one. It signals your child's independence and triggers the realization that he will never again need you quite as completely.

Pediatricians generally suggest babies use a cup for most of their liquids by the time they're a year old. We also live in a society that generally frowns on breast-feeding older babies. Mothers I know who are still breast-feeding at 18 months and beyond are often defensive, sometimes even secretive, about nursing their babies.

When I took Jesse in for a regular checkup at nine months, his pediatrician suggested I begin to think about weaning. In the tenth month, she recommended we be down to three times a day, twice a day at eleven months, and once a day during the twelfth month.

By the end of the first year, she said, my breast milk would not supply him with adequate amounts of protein, potassium, or other nutrients, and he would need cow's milk or formula.

I'd had little success when I tried supplementing Jesse's breast milk with formula during the first nine months, and I expressed to the pediatrician my concern that he would not get enough milk when I began to wean him from the breast.

First, she recommended I try a toddler formula, which is sweeter and tastes more like breast milk. If that didn't work, she said, it was all right to go ahead and offer cow's milk as a supplement. If he accepted the cow's milk, however, I might need to give him an over-the-counter iron supplement unless I felt he was getting sufficient iron from meats and vegetables served during mealtimes.

She also suggested I make sure to include other dairy products, like yogurt and cottage cheese, in his diet.

Weaning, our pediatrician said, should be a gradual process for both my sake and his and should not be attempted during unusual times of stress or upheaval, like a move or a vacation.

Many babies, she said, are "self weaners" and will gradually decrease their intake of breast milk with little or no guidance from Mom, especially if a stressful situation is not created by an overanxious mother. If this self-weaning is going to happen, it is most likely to occur between nine and twelve months.

"Weaning is just sort of happening on its own," said Anne when her daughter, Tori, was 11 months old. "I knew it would eventually be necessary, so as it began to happen, I just keyed into it. At first it was every two hours on demand, then she was on a regular schedule of five times a day, at about the same time each day."

Anne said she worked on one feeding at a time, substituting a cup of milk for each nursing episode she discontinued. "Our most recent one to go was right before bedtime, and that was the hardest for me to give up. I really enjoyed holding her close and cuddling her and smelling her right after her bath."

Weaning, Anne said, was not as traumatic as giving Tori her first solid foods. "At that point, I still wanted to be the one and only for her, to be all she needed in the world."

By eleven months, they were down to a morning and an afternoon feeding, and Tori was drinking three cups of milk, along with juice and water, every day. "I don't know if it is exactly a cup—eight ounces, I mean. I am not really measuring it, but I give her as much as she will drink from a cup," Anne said.

"They tell you when they are ready. She never cried or got hysterical, so I just kept on going," Anne said. "I just watched her body, and if she seemed healthy and happy, I didn't worry."

I, too, wanted to avoid the emotional trauma so often associated with weaning. To do this, I knew I would have to be sensitive enough to follow Jesse's lead, to pay attention to the cues that would tell me when the time was right.

Jesse's interest in nursing decreased and increased at different times. It diminished when he started to crawl but picked up again when he had a growth spurt a month or so later. Teething would also affect his need to nurse, sometimes increasing and at other times decreasing his demand.

When he began to cruise along the furniture with such intense concentration that he forgot his midmorning feeding two days in a row, I saw this as an opportunity to abandon this feeding altogether. So I would not also lose the time we spent together during that midmorning nursing, I substituted a game, a book, or a walk outside to examine bugs, flowers, blades of grass, and other wonders of the world I had long taken for granted.

Dropping the late-afternoon feeding was a little more difficult. Jesse was noticeably crankier in the afternoon, even though I offered him a snack (usually some cubes of fruit; a slice of processed cheese or some cottage cheese or yogurt; a cracker or a cookie; and a glass of milk) in place of the abandoned breast-feeding. It seemed to be the comfort that he missed rather than the breast milk itself.

His normal sleeping pattern was also disrupted for a couple of weeks while we adjusted to the new three-nursings-a-day schedule. He would wake at 4:30 every morning and refuse to go back to sleep until around 6 A.M., just when it was time for me to get up, of course.

The first couple of mornings, I did what the pediatrician and most baby experts recommend you not do: I slipped him into bed with us and let him have his morning nip a couple of hours early. When this seemed to be developing into a pattern, I got tough and let him cry himself back to sleep for the next couple of mornings, until we resumed a more restful schedule.

I can't say with certainty that the weaning process affected his sleep, but the two events began on the same day, which seems too great a coincidence to ignore.

BOUNCING THE BABY, AND THE CHECKBOOK

If you thought having the baby was expensive—in most cases, about $10,000 for prenatal care and a normal delivery—wait until your little darling discovers Toys 'R' Us.

There were more than 4 million babies born in the United States in 1994, according to the U.S. Census Bureau. About a third of them were born to women in their thirties, primarily into affluent, double-income families. This represents a vast market for the manufacturers of baby clothes, shoes, toys, furniture, and a host of other things I have yet to imagine.

Like most upscale career women who have become new mothers in a decade of conspicuous consumption, I have fallen prey to the brand-name game. I am more familiar with the top names in baby clothing—Gymboree, babyGap, Patagonia and Baby Guess?—than I am with adult labels. Baby must have the best (well, the best my bank account can afford), the cutest, the most chic, while I am now shopping the blue-light specials at K-Mart.

My mother recently said to me, "Now you know why I never bought anything for myself when you kids were growing up. I'd much rather buy for you." I'm glad she still feels that way, otherwise I might never get anything new to wear.

I am also now listed as a "favored customer" by most of the children's catalogs. They are filled with delightful things to tempt me—toys that will make my child brighter, devices that will keep him safer, and innumerable other items to make life with Baby a little easier.

A lot of the items—the thirty dollar interactive soft books designed for babies who are still more interested in eating a book than reading it, or teddy bears, also about thirty dollars, that make soothing, intrauterine sounds—are destined to trigger the guilt factor, especially for working parents who live by the "Quality, if not quantity" motto.

When I hired a baby-sitter for several days so I could work uninterrupted on a special project, I celebrated the completion with a trip to the toy store, where I loaded the cart with an assortment of things that squeaked, rattled, beeped, and bounced. They all made me very happy. Jesse liked the boxes.

A year ago, I would have bought myself a dress, or tucked the bonus cash away toward the purchase of an airplane ticket to someplace tropical.

Month eleven

PRIMORDIAL SCREAMS

Some mothers find the eleventh month to be the most difficult time of the year—a time when they may be more apt to lose control and lash out at their child in anger and frustration.

Older babies don't cry as much, don't need diaper and clothing changes as often, don't eat every two hours, and are probably sleeping through the night most of the time. So why should this part of the year be more difficult for a mother?

The average baby begins to cruise along the furniture or walk at about 11 months of age. Keeping up with a baby on the move can frazzle even the calmest, most composed of mothers. Jesse took his first steps the night before his eleventh-month "birthday," and this marked the beginning of a whole new adventure for all of us. As he got stronger, smarter, and more mobile, he had to be watched every waking moment or confined to a playpen, where he would scream until he was once again free to roam.

His increasing mobility revealed an exciting, unprecedented view of his world. He was much more dexterous and could open cabinets and drawers, unscrew the knobs from the pasta machine, and crank up the volume on the stereo to an earsplitting level. Suddenly, he could get his hands on all the things I thought I had moved out of his reach. A few months earlier, he knew the command "No" and obeyed it most of the time. At eleven months, he seemed to enjoy challenging me on every no I uttered with his own "na-na-na-na."

An 11-month-old child can unprogram the television remote control so that you have to pay twenty dollars for a cable service technician to come out and untangle the mess, or spend three hours trying to decipher the operator's manual yourself. He can pull a bottle of maple syrup down from the pantry, carry it into the living room, and pour it onto the carpet. He can reach the keyboard of your computer and delete hours of work.

He can drive you crazy, push you to the abysmal brink of sanity, where your only release is a scream that comes from ancestral depths, something not quite civilized. You will wonder whose voice it was and where it came from, but you'll feel a little better once it has been purged from your system.

The end of the year is an in-between stage for both mother and child. Jesse was no longer a compliant baby totally dependent on me. He had a mind and a will of his own, but he was not yet a sensible child who could be responsible for his own actions and trusted not to get into dangerous situations in the blink of an eye.

On the one hand, he still needed my love and emotional support as much as ever, if not more. On the other hand, he fought the physical control I continued to wield over him, constantly challenging me when I changed a diaper, put on his clothes, or took some object away from him.

I want my son to grow up to be an independent, self-reliant adult who knows what he wants and goes about getting it with forthright determination. These qualities in an 11-month-old child, however, can push the limit of any mother's patience and sanity. There were several times, as our first year was drawing to a close, when I felt myself on the verge of losing control.

Only the mothers I know really well admit to yelling at their babies. But I suspect most mothers have yelled on at least a few occasions, despite their intention to always speak softly and calmly—especially during the first tender year of their child's life.

"I have made a conscious effort with my speech, to keep it even toned no matter what. I don't want to teach my son to yell, and he learns from what he sees and hears us do," Chalene said. "The only time I ever raised my voice in that first year was to yell at the dogs. When Skyler began to talk, the first thing he did was scream at the dogs. I guess, as a parent, you are going to slip sometimes, no matter how conscientious you think you are."

Lisa, another of my mentor moms, was quick to acknowledge that she has screamed at her baby, now a toddler, many times. "You'll do it, and then you'll feel bad about it."

To avoid descending to your child's immature level, Lisa said, you have to stop, take a deep breath and ask yourself why you are feeling so angry. If you can calm yourself long enough to ask that question and to think about the situation, you can probably control the anger, she said.

Most of the time, she added, it is not what your child is doing at the moment that really angers you, but a culmination of the day's events.

"Maybe you had a bad day at work, or you are mad at

your husband. Maybe your kid wouldn't go to bed the night before, and you didn't get enough sleep," Lisa continued. "Whatever the reason, you may just be right on the edge and unable to keep yourself from going over."

The feeling, many mothers agree, is like falling from a cliff—you want to pull yourself back, but once you've begun the tumble, you just keep gathering momentum until you hit bottom.

"Any mother who tells you she has never yelled at her child is either lying or on lithium," Lisa added.

Lisa struggled with tremendous hormonal imbalances following the birth of her daughter. Birth-control shots pushed her beyond the limit of her ability to cope, and her doctor prescribed medication to calm her nerves.

"I just wanted everyone to go away and leave me alone. I didn't even want them to look at me," Lisa said, recalling how she reacted to her family during those months. "Now I take Prozac, and I don't yell at my child anymore. Now, when she does something that would have sent me into orbit, I can remain calm and reason with her. She'll look at me so intently and listen because I'm not screaming at her."

At the beginning of this motherhood business, I too had promised myself never to yell at Jesse in anger. I kept that promise for most of the first year. (Screaming "No!" or "Stop!" just before he grabs a hot cup of coffee does not count.)

I broke the promise just before our eleventh month when, at the end of a very long day, I lost all control and found myself screaming, "Stop it, stop it, stop it!" at the top of my lungs. I vaguely recall stomping my feet as well.

Jesse had been cranky and whiny, refusing to eat his cereal at breakfast or take an afternoon nap when I needed to get laundry done. He had stuffed most of a roll of toilet paper down the commode and ripped the grillwork from a stereo speaker. In both instances, I was only a few feet away but couldn't see what he was doing with his hands. I was angry at myself for not keeping a more watchful eye on him.

I'm sure he didn't know that the last straw for me would be the fit he threw when I put him in his high chair so I could prepare his dinner. Of course, my screaming didn't help matters. It just turned his annoying whine into a terrified wail and made me feel incredibly guilty. I worried that I had done irreparable damage to his psyche. I don't want him to end up in therapy, blaming his mother for his insecurities.

I wondered about my own sanity. Did this loss of control mean I was not a good mother, or just that Mommy needed a little time out herself?

"This is not abnormal," said Lou Strain, Faulkner County director for Counseling Associates, a multi-county mental health agency operating in central Arkansas. "Losing your cool is not what I consider abusive parenting; that is a parent needing help, needing a break."

Strain has worked extensively with abused and emotionally disturbed children. During her years as director of a shelter for abused children, she witnessed many cases where mothers snapped and crossed the line from yelling to real abuse.

"It is not abnormal to want to shake or yell at your baby. What is abnormal is if you actually do it, if you cross that line," she said.

The way I felt reminded me of my grandmother's pressure cooker. When the steam built up inside the cooker, the weight on the top would jiggle, making a startlingly loud sound—a lot like my voice when I yelled at my son. I guess I was just releasing a little pressure. Like that cooker, if I don't want to explode, I'll have to learn to turn down the heat or take the pot off the stove.

"This is a sign that you need to change something in your life. It's a very personal thing. Get a sitter, go visit your parents for a few days, take a vacation. What works for one mother might not work for another," Strain said. "Sometimes all you need is a short-term remedy."

She recalled a young mother she counseled, a self-referral who was having serious problems dealing with her year-old child. "She had not been away from this child, not even to go to the grocery store by herself, for a year. Her husband was a jerk who would not help her; she had no parents, no support group. I congratulated her that she had survived as long as she did."

Strain said this was "an easy case. All we had to do was give her a break. Whenever you start to feel all this stress and pressure build up, you need to ask yourself, 'When was the last time I was away from this child?'"

Anytime there is a lack of sleep, the absence of an adequate support system, and a change in the daily routine, there will be stress, Strain continued. Add to this some new financial pressures and new responsibilities and you have the potential for trouble.

"All those things are part of being a new mother. Parenting is set up to stress you out, and we react to stress in a hundred different ways," she said. "One of those ways is to verbalize our stress, to yell at our kid."

New babies, she continued, are "100 percent narcissistic. That's how they survive. They just take and take from you and give little back. Babies are totally dependent, and most people are not prepared to deal with that. We are used to give-and-take relationships."

Mothers today, she said, have access to a lot more information and assistance than was available when she had her daughter twenty-one years ago. "We had one car, and my husband used it to get to work. Even if there had been some program, a mother's day out, I had no transportation. I was trapped at home with my baby, isolated with no outlets. This was a high-risk situation. If I hadn't had good parents as role models and a supportive husband, my child would have been at risk."

Strain recalled her first six weeks at home with her daughter. "She got her days and nights mixed up, and I was getting an average of two hours of sleep a day. One night, she woke me up at midnight, and I remember thinking, 'I'm going to kill her.' Luckily, my husband woke up too, saw my face, and tended to the baby."

What she didn't realize, because she didn't have much information at that point, was that her baby didn't have to be in total control of their sleeping schedule.

"When I took her in for the six-week checkup, the pediatrician told me not to let her sleep so much during the day and she would start sleeping better at night. It was as simple as that," she said.

The most important thing a new mom can do to keep the pressure from building to an explosive level is to establish an adequate support system.

"Your spouse can't always be there, so you need other people whom you can turn to for help. Find other new parents who can relate to what you are going through," Strain continued.

Go shopping, see a movie, take a walk, or visit the gym—whatever activity relaxes you the most. Don't use this free time for chores. Most important, accept that you are a mother, not a saint, and you are not always going to be June Cleaver—sweet and even-tempered with an ever-present smile on your face, the furniture dusted and cookies baking in the oven. Sometimes you are going to lose your cool and explode in a hailstorm of angry words. The best you can do is to say you're sorry and reassure your child that you love him.

HARD HATS AND SAFETY GOGGLES

Worry and stress inevitably conspire to undermine a new mother's cool demeanor, and few things can fray her nerves more quickly than a newly mobile, intensely curious child who is totally oblivious of danger.

Often when I lost it and either yelled at my son or had to put him into his playpen while I walked off and counted to ten, it was because he had done something, or a series of somethings, that truly frightened me. Things like pulling a small table over onto himself, yanking down the "child-proof" gate and climbing the stairs, or trying to swallow a handful of dog food. The anxiety created by a day filled with frightening near catastrophes can make even the most unflappable mother lose her composure.

When Jesse was 11 months old, I joked to family and friends that I needed to buy him a pint-sized helmet to protect his head from the constant falls and bumps and maybe a pair of junior goggles to deflect all those things that mothers say will put your eye out.

I was only half kidding. He seemed to almost always have a bruise on his forehead or chin. Each day there would be at least one incident of falling and bumping his head on either the floor or the furniture, or pinching a finger in a drawer or a cabinet door. Most of the time, these accidents left no real signs of damage, but some weeks he would look like he'd been playing hockey without a face mask.

Portrait sittings had to be rescheduled until a bruise had faded or a scratch healed, and I found myself quick to explain to friends, family members, and strangers alike how he got each little mark.

I wondered if people were beginning to suspect me of child abuse. Was I doing something wrong? Was I not being diligent enough? What could I do to avoid these mishaps?

"Rub it, kiss it, say some soothing words. That's all you really need to do for most minor bumps and bruises," said our pediatrician, adding that these accidents were normal at this stage, when a baby was just beginning to walk and had a healthy curiosity about his world.

"If the bump is on the head and there is swelling, put some ice on it," Dr. Ponzio continued. "Even if he's got an egg-sized lump, it shouldn't be a problem unless he passes out or vomits or if he cries inconsolably for more than ten or fifteen minutes. Then you call me."

If a hug and a kiss don't stop the tears, Dr. Ponzio said, a distraction, such as a favorite toy or book or a walk outside, might do the trick.

A mother must walk a fine line between reacting and overreacting. Your first instinct is to clutch your baby to your panting bosom and run around the room, screaming, "Oh, God! Oh, God!" Trust me, this is definitely not the appropriate behavior, because your baby will take his cue from your reaction and panic as well. If he is truly hurt, he will cry immediately, but if it's mostly his feelings that got damaged, he will watch for your reaction to judge how he should react himself.

Major mishaps, involving a lot of blood or loss of consciousness, naturally require quick action. There is little doubt about what you should do—dial 911! All those minor accidents, however, call for the perfect balance of reassuring calm and soothing support without unnecessary panic and agitation.

If I responded too quickly or with too much emotion, Jesse would take this as a signal to cry even harder, perhaps becoming frightened more by my response than the accident itself. If I delayed my reaction too long, however, he would become frustrated to the point of indignation.

Sometimes, when a fall bruised only his ego, I could tell Jesse was only offended by the misadventure and not quite certain if he should cry or not. If I laughed and clapped my hands as if he had just performed a really cute trick, this would often forestall any substantial crying jag and leave him laughing, too.

I thought I had childproofed our home sufficiently, but as Jesse began to pull up on the furniture and toddle those first unsteady steps, I discovered many hazards I had not anticipated. These included a top-heavy end table unsteady enough to tip over when Jesse used it to pull himself up, and a telephone with an extra long cord that dangled temptingly near his exploring grasp.

Another lesson was learned after Jesse pinched his fingers in the hinged side of a kitchen-cabinet door. I had left most of the kitchen cabinets unlatched because they contained lightweight pots, pans, and plastics that were not off-limits to the baby. What I did not anticipate, however, was that Jesse would open the cabinet and then shut the door on his fingers. Latching all cabinet doors or using hinge protectors will eliminate this risk.

No matter how well you have babyproofed your house, the best safety measure is never to leave your child unattended. Even when you are by his side, minor bumps and bruises will occur, but constant diligence and a few common-sense precautions will reduce the odds of more serious injury. Here are a few more specific safety tips, based on my own experience and warnings from other mothers:

- Treat knives, screwdrivers, and other sharp objects—
  even pencils—with extreme caution once your baby
  is able to easily grasp everything within his reach. (A
  baby's reach, by the way, is much longer than you
  think.) I narrowly averted a serious accident with a
  knife one afternoon when I sat Jesse on the kitchen
  counter to watch me prepare his dinner. I had left a
  handful of silverware drying on a towel by the sink.
  Before I had even turned him loose, he grabbed a
  sharp knife from the pile and stuck it into his
  mouth, nicking his fingers and scratching his cheek
  before I could get it away from him.

- Remove small, lightweight rugs from polished floors,
  especially near stairs; they can spell disaster for a toddler already doing a balancing act on unsteady feet.

- Never underestimate your child's ability to fall head-
  first from a bed or a table, even when you are at his
  side. Jesse took his first high dive when he was 10
  months old and fell from the changing table. He
  had dropped a toy to the floor, and when I leaned to
  the left to retrieve it, he sat up and leaned to my
  right. I was able to catch him and break the fall
  before he landed on the floor but not before he
  struck his mouth on the shelf, causing his gums to
  bleed and his lip to swell.

In another instance, Jesse fell from the bed in a hotel
room and scratched his chest on a piece of metal protruding
from the bed frame.

By the time her daughter was 11 months old, Anne had
taught Tori to turn around and back off a bed or couch to

get to the floor. This, she said, prevented many a bump and bruise. "We had worked on it a long time, and finally, one day, something clicked in her little mind, and she just did it on her own."

- It is also a good idea to teach your baby how to back down stairs, even though he is much too young ever to be allowed to climb the stairs without your help.
- Don't let your crawling or walking baby amble about in socks without shoes, unless the socks have rubber soles or all of your floors are carpeted; socks on tile or linoleum are a slippery combination.
- Never leave plastic bags within your baby's reach. For some inexplicable reason, babies seem to be irrepressibly drawn to the very things that pose the most danger to them. I kept a collection of plastic grocery bags on the changing-table shelf for months, until I read about the baby who suffocated after his mother inadvertently left just such a bag lying on the crib mattress.

Especially hazardous is the filmy plastic used by dry cleaners. It should be disposed of as soon as you get home—without hesitation. On a typical afternoon, I entered the house with the cleaning draped over my shoulder, a bag of groceries on one arm, and Jesse on the other. I hung the cleaning on a coat rack by the door and settled Jesse on the floor. Before I could put down the groceries and take off my coat, he had ripped off a piece of the plastic and stuffed it into his mouth. If I hadn't been watching, if I hadn't been only a few steps away, it could have been fatal.

- Frequently use words and phrases like *hot* and *don't touch* to warn your baby about the dangers of the stove, the fireplace, or a steaming cup of coffee. We were having dinner out with friends and the waitress had just poured a fresh cup of coffee when Jesse grabbed for the cup and stuck his hand into the hot liquid. Harold, in a moment of quick thinking, plunged the baby's hand into a nearby glass of ice water. There were plenty of tears, but no blisters from the ordeal.

On another occasion, I had Jesse perched on my left hip and was pouring a cup of coffee with my right hand, being careful to keep the cup and the pot out of his reach. He grabbed for the coffee maker instead, toasting his fingers on the warming element that the pot sits on. Again, cold water was the best remedy.

- Put away your tablecloths and place mats, since both can allow your child to pull something down from the table. Tracy's son, Nathan, managed to get his hands on a bottle of cough syrup by tugging on a tablecloth. The bottle was emptied all over a white carpet, but Tracy was just grateful he didn't drink the contents.

"They learn so quickly. Things that were safe yesterday are not safe today," Tracy said. "He is into absolutely everything, and he just won't give up until he gets what he wants."

- In the nursery, make sure the crib slats are no more than $2\frac{3}{8}$ inches apart and there are no sharp edges or cutouts that your baby can get an arm, leg, or head stuck in. Make sure the crib mattress fits securely, with no gaps, and remove the plastic cover from the mattress. An older, mobile baby would have no problem pulling sheets and mattress covers out of the way to get to the dangerous plastic underneath.

- Buy or make a guard for your fireplace hearth. Bumpers specially designed for that purpose can be purchased at children's stores or through specialty catalogs. For some hearths, a quilt or a folded rug will do. A friend's daughter was just a little over a year old when she fell against a sharp-edged brick hearth, leaving a gash across her forehead that required several stitches and an emergency-room visit. Tables with glass tops or sharp corners should also be padded or removed.

- Bathrooms are particularly hazardous places for a crawling or walking baby, so the best advice is to keep the door securely closed. Doorknob covers may be needed when your toddler learns how to turn the knob. Even if you plan always to keep the bathroom door secured, it's also a good idea to put locks on the toilet seat. Jesse, like most babies his age, cannot resist playing in the water, and it would be easy for him to fall forward and drown. Medicines, vitamins, and cosmetics, usually kept in bathrooms, should be stored in high, preferably locked cabinets.

- Elsewhere around the house, chemicals, paints, solvents, dangerous tools, and other hazardous materials generally found in garages should be locked up,

swimming pools should be fenced in, and house-
plants should be moved out of reach or removed
entirely if they are toxic.

Because you can expect accidents to happen, no matter
how careful you are, it is also wise to keep a good first-aid kit
handy and an ice pack in the freezer. Our pediatrician also
advised us to keep syrup of ipecac, which induces vomiting,
in the medicine chest, but warned us not to use it without
first checking with a doctor or the poison control center.

Knowing the number of the poison control center is
wise even if you don't have children, a must if you do. There
are more than sixty different centers around the United
States, but no national 800 number, so find out what the
toll-free number is in your specific region by checking the
telephone book or calling information. Brochures and pam-
phlets listing poisonous plants and other toxic substances
and stickers listing the appropriate telephone number to call
in an emergency are available at these centers.

Paul McNeese, with the Los Angeles Regional Drug
and Poison Information Center, said separate centers are
needed in different parts of the country because each
region has its own unique hazards. The Los Angeles center,
one of the largest in the country, handles approximately
130,000 calls a year.

"Sixty-five percent of all accidental poisonings occur to
children under the age of 6. They are illiterate, curious, and
oral," McNeese said.

Keeping your baby out of danger is one of your greatest
responsibilities as a new mother, and the best way to prepare for the task is to arm yourself with as much information as possible.

Emergency Reaction

Your baby has just swallowed a luscious-looking red berry he plucked from a shrub by the back door. What should you do—call 911, or the local poison control center?

"There are some very simple rules to follow when your baby has been exposed to a poison or when you think he may have been," said Paul McNeese, spokesman for the Los Angeles Regional Drug and Poison Information Center.

You should always call 911 first if the baby exhibits any of the following symptoms:

- He is not breathing or is having trouble breathing.

- He is unconscious, or in and out of consciousness.

- He is having convulsions or seizures of any kind.

- He suddenly becomes pale and cold.

- He is either very limp or very stiff.

"In most cases, 911 calls us and puts us on the phone with the caller while the ambulance is on the way," McNeese said. If you detect none of the symptoms listed above, call the poison control center first. Don't wait for symptoms to develop.

Often, he said, parents can manage the situation at home, or they have plenty of time to take their child to the emergency room themselves. If an ambulance is needed, the poison control center will call 911 or direct the parents to make the call.

Accidental poisoning will be one of your greatest fears during your first year as a mother. Prevention is the best way to deal with this potential for disaster, but you should still be prepared for such an emergency no matter how well you think you have babyproofed your home and yard.

After removing toxic plants and locking away chemicals and other poisonous substances, the best thing you can do is have handy the telephone number for the local poison control center and be prepared to react calmly in an emergency.

Most telephone books have the number on the community pages or under an emergency or medical-services listing. Because the centers are independent, there is not a great deal of consistency in how they are listed. Some are under the auspices of the county, while others are city or state affiliated. If you have trouble finding the number in the telephone book, call information for assistance.

Most poison control centers have stickers printed with their emergency telephone number which they will gladly mail to you, along with various brochures on poisoning prevention.

If the worst happens despite your best efforts at prevention, be prepared before you call the poison control center. Your memory may be impaired by your fear and anxiety, so have a pencil and paper handy to write down instructions. If your baby ingested or came into contact with a chemical, bring the container to the telephone with you and be ready to give the following information:

- Name of victim, age, sex, and weight.

- Name of substance or substances involved.

- Type of exposure: ingestion, inhalation, eye, or skin contact.

- How long since exposure.

- Amount of substance involved or length of time in contact.

- What treatment (e.g. vomiting) or first-aid has been given.

- What symptoms the victim has.

WEATHERING THE TEMPEST

Comforting a crying child who has fallen down or pinched an exploring finger is a task mothers learn to do without much thought. It becomes almost instinctive with time. What we never quite get used to dealing with is a temper tantrum. The only thing worse than a temper tantrum is a temper tantrum in a public place or when your in-laws are visiting.

Like separation and stranger anxiety, temper tantrums are a normal part of a child's development, and most mothers will have to learn to cope with them.

"Few mothers can avoid them entirely," Dr. Ponzio said. "You just have to get used to it, try to be a model of calm during them, and provide a lot of distractions. Food is good."

Children at this age, she said, are easily distracted. If your child is playing with the telephone, move it out of sight and give him something else. In a couple of minutes, he will have forgotten about the telephone. Just try to remember where you hid it so you don't have to go on a scavenger hunt the next time you want to make a call.

If you can't move the object of his attention, move the baby, Dr. Ponzio said. Again, within a few minutes, he will have forgotten all about the stairs he wanted to climb or the oven door he was pounding on with both hands.

Temper tantrums occur most often when something is taken away from the child, when he is told no in response to a certain action, and when he is overtired or overstimulated.

"Often, they forget why they started crying in the first place but just keep crying anyway. You can offer them something else, try to distract them, but sometimes this doesn't work, and all you can do is keep them safe," Dr. Ponzio said.

Easier said than done if you have a "head-banger" who bounces his cranium off the floor or crashes into walls during the tantrum. Equally as distressing for a new mom is an angry baby who holds his breath and passes out from lack of oxygen.

"If they are banging their head or thrashing about uncontrollably, you just have to hold them until they wear themselves out," Dr. Ponzio said. "Holding their breath is not abnormal, although it is unusual. It is not dangerous, but it is very frightening for the mother. You just have to ignore it. Don't reward the behavior."

Dr. Ponzio said her husband, a family practitioner, was unnerved the first time he witnessed a 2-year-old passing out during a tantrum in his office. "The mother was calm, but he freaked out because he had never seen this happen before," Dr. Ponzio said.

Some children experience their first temper tantrum before they are a year old, although the average age for this phase to begin is around two years.

"That's why they call it the terrible twos," Dr. Ponzio said. "And like most of the other stages, they will eventually outgrow this one, as well, usually by the time they are 4 or 5."

Kim's daughter, Chelsea, was 10 months old and just learning to walk when she began having temper tantrums. "Whenever I told her to leave something alone, or if I walked away from her, she would get so mad and cry so hard that she'd pass out."

Their pediatrician assured her Chelsea would outgrow this phase, and by the time she was 2½, the instances were rare, but that doesn't dim the unpleasant memory of that traumatic first time.

"I called 911. I was so scared. She was turning blue, but as soon as she passed out, she started to breath again," Kim recalled. "It was always frightening, but we got used to it. There wasn't anything else we could do. It happened every time she got angry or frightened."

Temper tantrums, the pediatrician said, are not necessarily bad. When children become frustrated, when their emotions become overloaded, they need some sort of release. A mother should be concerned about a temper tantrum only if the child is unresponsive to normal social cues and does not seem to want her attention during the episode. This kind of behavior, she said, could be a sign of autism.

Olympic Tryouts

In the eleventh month, you will spend much of your day feeding and cleaning, soothing bumps and bruises, and trying to keep your baby's frustration below the temper-tantrum level. In your "spare" time, you'll be playing games and struggling to remember the nursery rhymes of your own childhood.

Having spent little time around babies, I must confess to a total ignorance of baby games and nursery rhymes. Peekaboo I could figure out on my own, but I didn't know the words to "Pop Goes the Weasel" or "Patty Cake" (or is that "Pat-a-Cake"?).

It was a little embarrassing to ask more experienced moms to recite for me the words to "This little piggy went to market" and "One, two, buckle my shoe." In retrospect, it probably would have been a good idea to buy a few books of nursery rhymes and baby games while I was still pregnant and had the time to read.

Games not only provide hours of fun and entertainment for you and your baby, they also teach skills and concepts, coordinate words with actions, and improve socialization. And by the end of the day, you'll have had a workout worthy of an Olympic hopeful.

Up until this point, the park days and play groups were mostly for my benefit, to give me the support of other mothers. At eleven months, Jesse needed the interaction of other children as much as I needed time with adults.

One of the best sources I found for learning about games and nursery rhymes was an organized play group appropriate for Jesse's age.

"My kids have grown up in this program. We haven't participated in several months, and they are going through withdrawal," said Michele, mother of a 2-year-old and a 6-year-old, and an instructor for a local play program.

"We work on concepts and colors, and each week we have a new theme for songs. It's great for kids because they learn how to act around a group and how to share. And it's good for parents because you learn all those games and songs that you probably haven't heard in decades."

SPLISH, SPLASH

Equally as important as playtime is bath time. In fact, your baby's bath may sometimes be the most enjoyable part of the day. All of my mentor moms agree: Babies, especially older babies who can sit up without support, love to play and splash in the bath.

No matter how fussy he had been at dinner or how offended he was at me for saying no a dozen times the previous hour, Jesse always had a big smile for me during his bath. Even teething discomfort seemed to be forgotten in the wake (you can take that literally, as well as figuratively) of a tub filled with warm, bubbly water.

I had been bathing for years and considered myself quite an expert at the task. How could bathing a baby be all that difficult?, I asked myself before Jesse was born. If only I had known how much I didn't know about the fine art of bathing a baby. There should be a class, a seminar, maybe even graduate studies on the subject.

We started out in the kitchen sink—just big enough and the right height to keep my back from aching. It was a challenge, though, to keep a firm grip on his wet, wiggling body, and I was always afraid he would slip out of my grasp. Then I tried setting a small, plastic baby bath on the bathroom vanity, and this proved to be the most efficient method until he was about 6 months old and could sit up on his own. Then we returned to the kitchen sink, where he could sit on a rubber mat without slipping and sliding around.

One of the things I learned early on was always to run the bath water before putting the baby into the tub or sink. Sudden changes in water pressure (someone flushing a toilet elsewhere in the house, for instance) can create a burst of hot water. Babies love to turn knobs and handles, and I also learned quickly that it is wise to swivel the faucet away from the baby in case he turns the hot water on full blast.

You should always test the water first, using your elbow rather than your hands. I had heard this sage advice from other mothers, but I forgot—or chose to ignore—the admonishment in a fog of weariness one evening. The water felt just right to my fingers, but my hands had been under the running water for some time and had grown accustomed to the temperature. When I eased Jesse into the water, he howled in outrage until I quickly removed him. When I tested the water with my elbow, I realized it was much too hot for that delicate baby tush.

Of course we had the obligatory rubber ducky, but some of the most fun bath toys I found were not purchased at the toy store. They came out of the kitchen: a turkey baster, a funnel, measuring cups, and drinking glasses (all plastic, of course). A clean sponge that can be squeezed, tossed, dunked, and sucked on is also a bath-time treat for your baby.

I continued to use the kitchen sink for an occasional quick cleanup, but we graduated to the big bathtub around the end of the year. Bath rings and seats that help keep baby from slipping and sliding around are a big help. A kneeling pad or a rolled-up towel will help prevent knee pain for Mom.

Keep plenty of towels on hand—one to dry baby, one to sit baby on while you dry him off, and one to keep the floor dry. A wet tile floor can be a hazard for both of you. I slipped on a wet kitchen floor after one of Jesse's evening baths. I didn't drop the baby or fall completely to the floor, but I did pull a muscle that ached for days afterward.

Like most mothers, I started out bathing Jesse in the mornings. It seemed like a nice way to start the day, and besides, during the first few months, he usually wet through his diaper during the night. As he got older and began to crawl, cruise, and eventually walk all over the house, on the patio, and in the garage (under supervision, of course), it became obvious that an evening bath was a necessity. Some days, we took a lot of baths.

"Actually, Tori gets two baths a day, every day. She likes bath time so much, we do one in the morning and another at night," Anne said, adding that the evening bath had become part of the bedtime ritual. "It really relaxes her and helps her go to sleep on her own."

My final word on bath time is one every mother hears over and over again, but never too often: Don't leave your baby unattended in the bathtub, not even for a few seconds. It only takes a fraction of that time for a baby to slip and crack his head on the hard surface of the tub or fall facedown and inhale a mouthful of water. Even when your baby is old enough to sit on his own and doesn't need to be held constantly, you should still be within arm's length. If you can't stand to let the telephone ring, take a portable one into the bathroom with you or buy an answering machine. And put a note on the door that says, "Bathing baby, come back later."

ON GOLDEN THRONE

Since we're already in the bathroom for bathing, now seems a good time to discuss toilet training. By all accounts (from pediatricians and mothers), the end of the first year is much too early to begin toilet training, but it was not too soon for me to begin thinking about setting the stage for the endeavor to come some six to twelve months down the road.

When Jesse was just shy of his 10-month birthday, my mother began to gently but persistently prod me about toilet training. In talking with other new moms, I have found that their mothers also seem to recall babies who walked at seven months, were potty trained at ten months, and had a full vocabulary by the end of the year, as well as a mouthful of teeth. Obviously, their memories have been embellished by time, or they all had unusually perfect children.

"Ten months is way too young to even begin toilet training," the pediatrician advised. "You've got too much else going on right now, so don't even think about it. Most boys are not completely potty trained until they are 3 years old. Between 18 months and 2 years, you should buy a potty chair and leave it in the bathroom, just so they can get used to seeing it.

"Before you can start, he is going to have to be talking and must have some awareness of his bodily functions," Dr. Ponzio said. Most babies aren't even aware when they have soiled or wet themselves until they are a year old. It will be well into the second year, she said, before they can anticipate the need to do either.

Even though it was much too early to begin toilet training, I reasoned that it couldn't hurt to at least let Jesse become familiar with basic bathroom etiquette. I often carried him into the bathroom with me instead of sticking him in his playpen and would draw his attention to the sound of my water passing. I would let him flush the toilet and watch the contents swirl away—and was usually successful at keeping his hands out of the bowl during the process.

If I caught the cue that he was about to have a bowel movement (red, straining face and a concentrated grunt or two), I would tell him what he was doing and show him the proceeds of his endeavors when I changed his diaper. On a few rare occasions, I could do the same when he urinated. It's almost impossible to tell when a baby is urinating, although sometimes I could detect a slight shiver from Jesse during the act. More often the opportunity presented itself when Jesse was taking a bath or romping naked by the pool.

Somehow I never imagined myself (in this idealistic, madonnalike vision I had of motherhood) spending my days watching for signs of poopoo and weewee.

SOMEONE'S BEEN SLEEPING IN MY BED

Having my son share the privacy of my bathroom was not something I anticipated while pregnant. Nor did I contemplate having him share the intimacy of my bed. Of course I had read and heard about the "family bed," a controversial subject with intense feelings on both sides. For a while, it was a hot topic, and you couldn't channel surf without catching proponents and opponents tangling on a television talk show.

Parents who favor the family bed say their children sleep much better and wake less often. Those who oppose it, however, claim just the opposite, contending that children who sleep with their parents have higher instances of sleep disorder.

Like many of the mothers I have talked with during the year, I was certain I would not want to share this space with anyone but my husband. And, like many of those same mothers, I changed my mind the instant I brought my son home from the hospital.

It was a delicious feeling when he was an infant, that warm body snuggled up against me, close enough to hear his breath and feel his heart beating. Even now, as he nears his first birthday, I still bask in that closeness and find it all too tempting to nestle him beside me at the end of the day.

I often brought Jesse into our bed when he was still breast-feeding during the night. Even when he was 7 and 8 months old, it often seemed easier when he woke crying just to slip him into our bed, rather than spend half an hour trying to settle him back into his own crib. I knew that what I was doing might not be the best thing, but all I could think about at the time was getting my own head back down on a pillow.

"Just do what's practical," our pediatrician advised. "At the beginning of the year, for most mothers, it is practical to bring the baby into their bed for nighttime feedings and just leave him there. If it helps you get some rest, that's what's important."

During the second half of the year, Dr. Ponzio said, cosleeping is still OK "as long as it is not interfering with your sleep or your relationship with your husband. Proponents and opponents quote all kinds of facts, but I've not seen any scientific evidence to indicate it helps or hurts.

It's not going to warp your baby, but if you are not getting any rest, it's not a good idea."

I would probably have no qualms about his sleeping with us if I didn't fear it would eventually infringe on our own privacy. There is a big difference between having an infant sharing your bed and a toddler snuggling between you. And the older he got, the more disruptive it was to both my sleep and my husband's.

When Jesse is in the bed with us, I sleep much lighter and will wake if he makes a small sound or changes position. Even Harold, who has slept through several California earthquakes, has had his slumber interrupted by Jesse's nighttime wiggling. On one occasion, Jesse's tears woke me around 3 A.M., and I slipped him into our warm bed, where we both promptly fell back into a peaceful slumber. Less than an hour later, I awoke to the sound of my husband's grumbling. Jesse was standing in the middle of the bed beating a staccato rhythm on his father's back and laughing with unsuppressed glee. What a fun game for a Sunday morning!

Although I usually enjoyed having Jesse in our bed, I never really wanted him to sleep there all of the time. Unfortunately, there does not seem to be a way to compromise between the two.

I want Jesse to know it is OK to be alone and to feel comfortable and safe in his own room. Besides, after spending most of my day catering to his needs, I often view those glorious hours between 9 P.M. and 6 A.M. as my sanctuary. I need that time to revitalize myself and to share with my husband.

Whichever choice you make, don't feel guilty if you deviate from time to time. If there is anything I have learned from this year, it is that you can't raise a child strictly by the book. You should have a plan, but you must realize that sometimes you will have to make exceptions.

Throughout the childhood years, Dr. Ponzio said, there will probably be sporadic times when I bring Jesse into our bed—during an illness, following a frightening or traumatic event, or sometimes just when it "feels right."

Month twelve

BITTERSWEET REFLECTIONS

My first year as a mother passed so quickly I was left with a surreal sensation that I hadn't seen any of it coming toward me—only glimpses of memorable moments flashing past me, as if in a rearview mirror.

I expected to feel a certain sense of celebration at the end of the first year. Didn't it mean we had reached a milestone? Wasn't it the moment we had been waiting for? Why did I feel like crying instead of rejoicing?

In many ways, the end of your child's first year is a bench mark. A 1-year-old child is less vulnerable than the newborn you brought home twelve months ago. You don't worry so much about crib death, colic, soft spots, and whether or not he is thriving. You are more self-assured as a mother, and you have the very obvious, determined-not-to-be-ignored evidence of a job well done waddling in your wake.

I adored the charming individual my son had become.

It was a relief not to agonize over the frailties of a newborn, not to worry if he was healthy and getting enough to eat. It was a relief not to unconsciously hold my breath every time I checked on him during the night, exhaling only after I was reassured that he was OK.

But even as I felt this magnitude of relief, a part of me missed the helpless little bundle whose existence had so overwhelmed me a year ago. I missed the pointy little bald head, the tiny fingers and curled-up toes. I missed the cry that sounded more like a kitten than a baby and the instinctive way he would turn his head to root at my breast every-time I picked him up.

Some of the women I have journeyed with down this maternal path said they also felt a bittersweet happiness as their baby's first birthday approached. Others expressed mostly relief and the sensation of a heavy burden being lifted.

"Everyone always looks forward to the first birthday. It's a big event, but I had mixed feelings," Kelli said, recalling her melancholy as she packed away Jordan's infant carrier and other baby things.

"I was relieved, excited, happy, and a little bit sad. It's hard to let go of your baby, to accept that he's now a toddler," Kelli said. "Looking back at the whole year, there is not a lot I would do differently. I wish I had breast-fed longer. I stopped after eight weeks, and I wish I had put more into it. There was a lot of social pressure to breast-feed, and I felt guilty that I didn't keep it up."

Another mistake Kelli said she wouldn't make again is to put too much emphasis on a first-birthday party. "The party was a real letdown," she recalled. "He wasn't excited—he was overwhelmed. We planned a big family dinner. It was late, and he was tired. We should have planned something more low-key, done it earlier in the day, and just ordered pizza."

Chalene echoed similar thoughts of mingled joy and sadness following her son's first birthday. "He's doing so many things now. It makes me sad." Even though she only hired a sitter four times during the first year, Chalene said she felt as if she had "missed a lot" because the year had been so hectic. Her father passed away after a lengthy illness, and she and her son spent most of his second six months traveling between California and her family home in Texas.

"I wish I could go back to six months, turn back the clock," Chalene said. "I wish I had done more with him. I'm not ready to graduate. I don't feel like I've passed a milestone. The realization that he is not a baby anymore makes me sad."

Hindsight is a truly wonderful thing. To begin the adventure of motherhood with about a year's worth of it would have been a blessing. Even though the other first-time mothers I have talked with during the year concurred, most of them said that they would change only a few things about the way they handled their baby and cared for their own needs during the year.

"For one thing, I would listen to my doctor," said Lisa. "I got up too soon, against my doctor's advice. I had a cesarean on Saturday, went home on Monday, and sent everyone packing on Tuesday. I thought I could do it all myself, without any help. I made it harder than it had to be. I had this vision that I had to be Supermom."

Lisa said she would also encourage her daughter to be more independent. "I would not pick her up every time she cried. I would not hold her and rock her to put her to sleep, because now she won't go to sleep on her own."

Most first-time mothers probably do this, Lisa speculated, because they have the time when there is only one child to tend. "It was easier on me when she was little, but it didn't do her any favors. It didn't teach her how to go to sleep on her own."

Establishing better sleep habits and breast-feeding for a longer time were the most common responses given when I asked other mothers if they had any major regrets about the first year.

"I would try to get him into a better sleep pattern earlier on," said Karen. "I stopped breast-feeding Garrett at three-and-a-half months because I thought formula might help him sleep longer at night. I didn't realize that waking throughout the night was just part of being a newborn. I thought it was all my fault. I was nervous about breast-feeding, and the more nervous I was, the more anxious he got."

Jennifer said she now regrets giving Collin a bottle to go to sleep at night. "It's a hard habit to break," she said. She also said she wishes she had gotten involved with a mother-and-baby play group when Collin was younger. "I meant to, but the time flies so quickly. Suddenly, he was a year old."

Isolating herself and "blowing off" social activities during the first few months is something else Jennifer said she might change a second time around. Most moms say they are so tied down by their baby's feeding and sleeping schedule that they barely have time to take a shower, much less get out of the house.

"I'm not really sure I would get out more in the early months. I think I needed that time alone with my baby," she said. "With a second child, I think you would have no choice. You would have to get out. But the first time around, it is hard. He had colic, and I didn't want to disturb other people with his crying. And John was gone five days a week for most of the year. It was hard to get out," she said.

"What I don't regret, though, is letting things go while he was a baby. I hear a lot of mothers say that they are sorry they spent so much time on housework instead of just sitting on the floor and playing with their baby," Jennifer said, adding that despite the colic and an absentee husband, she truly enjoyed the first year and "wouldn't trade it for anything. It was the loneliest time of my life, but it was also the happiest time of my life."

Anne, one of those lucky mothers who glowed during pregnancy and can't wait to do it again, viewed her daughter's first birthday as a mark of success. "I just felt like we made it. You worry so much about them that whole first year. Concern about SIDS (sudden infant death syndrome) was over. There had been no major injuries, no serious illnesses, not even an earache during the year."

Anne said she was just as busy, if not more so, caring for a 1-year-old as she had been when Tori was an infant, but even her husband noticed she was more relaxed.

"I felt like a burden had been lifted, and I didn't even know I had been carrying this burden around all year," Anne said. "Her first birthday gave me the chance to reevaluate myself, to realize and to acknowledge that I've done well, that I am really good at this mommy thing. It also changed the way I look at Tori. She's not just a project that has to be done; she's an individual person who shares our lives."

Anne said motherhood was easier than she had anticipated and more rewarding than she could ever have imagined. "I expected not to have time to take a shower or put makeup on or keep the house clean. I expected not to feel as romantic toward my husband, but my feelings were enhanced, magnified after Tori was born. I was prepared for it to be worse, and it wasn't. Maybe this was because Victoria was an easy baby, but I think a lot of it is in how you look at things, what you perceive to be easy or difficult."

She related the lamentations of another new mother

who struggled with breast-feeding and complained because she leaked milk and had to change breast pads frequently. "I had to wear breast pads too, but it didn't bother me. It was just part of it, like changing diapers," Anne said. "In the beginning, when I was leaking a lot, I put on a fresh breast pad every time I changed Tori's diaper. It became a routine."

Anne enjoyed her first year as a mother but described it as a time spent constantly trying to adjust to the new role and to keep pace with her baby's rapid changes.

"By her first birthday, I finally felt I had everything all caught up, even her baby book, and it was time to relax and enjoy the second year. I realized then, finally, that everything is not such a big deal. Babies get dirty; you can wash them. If their best clothes get stained, they just become play clothes."

Anne said she was comfortable with her style of mothering and couldn't think of anything she would do differently. "Maybe I wouldn't buy so many clothes. She has so many outfits and matching shoes and little hats that she's hardly wearing some of them. I'm starting to feel guilty about that, but they are so adorable."

In retrospect, several mothers also said they would try not to compare their child with other babies. While it is important to note your child's physical developments, too often mothers become overanxious if their baby does not weigh as much or doesn't crawl or walk as soon as a friend's baby.

Tracy, whose son was a late walker at fourteen months, said she tried to "block it out" when people would comment on this, or on his size. "It's hard not to feel defensive, because in your heart you think your child is perfect."

Karen also admitted comparing her son, Garrett, to other children but said it was "more out of curiosity than competition. When it's your first baby, you don't know what's normal, so you are always wondering."

I was guilty myself of making comparisons and fretted unnecessarily when a friend's daughter, three months younger than Jesse, outweighed him by several pounds. I was concerned that he wasn't eating enough. My pediatrician reassured me that his weight, height, and motor-skill development were all within the wide range of what is considered normal.

"Each baby is unique and will grow and develop differently. Comparisons can only result in unnecessary anxiety for the mother," she said. Mothers should not view their child's development as a race, but as a process that cannot be hurried by our expectations as parents or by the anticipation of others.

As Jesse's first birthday approached, I looked back on the year with a sense of satisfaction as well as relief. I treasure the memories of the good times, the tender, precious moments, but I also wear the struggles and hardships like a badge of honor. I grew as an individual and as a mother as a result of those difficult times. If I could repeat the year, start again from scratch, there are probably a thousand little things I would do differently, because I was constantly learning from my mistakes.

Mostly, I would try to relax and enjoy it more. The days I wore myself out trying to keep my head above a rising tide of dirty dishes, laundry, and housecleaning chores are best forgotten. The sweetest memories are from the lazy days I spent playing on the floor with my baby or taking him for a stroll in the park.

I would make a greater effort to silence the voices of guilt, those nagging little whispers that bounce around in my head whenever I left Jesse with a baby-sitter, whenever I did something totally selfish or self-serving, such as imprisoning him in a playpen so I could soak in a bubble bath. I would exercise until I banished that postpartum jelly belly. I would eat out more often. I would train my husband to do diapers.

I would not neglect my child's baby book. I waited six months to begin filling out Jesse's baby book. Even though I had made notes regularly and saved everything, it still took me three afternoons just to piece it all together. Six months later, I was scrambling to finish the second half of the book in time for the birthday party. The day-to-day demands of motherhood left me with little time or energy to chronicle all those precious firsts. I thought that I would remember each moment, but by the end of the year, I found my recollections a bit fuzzy around the edges.

Take photographs, make videos, and keep a mother's journal if you are ambitious. If you are less industrious, or maybe just more realistic about your time, keep a calendar in the nursery and jot down a few notes each day after you have changed a diaper or put your baby down for a nap. If you don't, you will regret it tremendously in later years or drive yourself nuts trying to reconstruct it all at the end of the year.

The first year of motherhood is a very special time that you will never get to repeat. Those mothers with two or more kids tell me that it is the only time they were able to devote full attention to their baby. As subsequent children came along, they found themselves with little time to delight in the inseparable intimacy of motherhood, much less take photographs and fill out baby books.

"With my first child, I did the traditional baby book and a photo album for the first year. With my second child, I bought a baby book but never got around to filling it out," said a mother of three. "My youngest is 8 months old now, and I haven't even had a studio photograph made."

The end of the first year is tinged with sadness but colored with hope and optimism that the coming year will only bring greater happiness and enrichment as you continue to evolve into the type of mother you want to be. You have made it through the transition period, and now is the time to make goals and set the tone for the future.

FLOWERING SPIRIT

If you could focus a time-lapse camera on a woman during her first year of motherhood, it would be like watching the petals of a flower gradually unfolding. Physically, I became a mother the night Jesse was born, but it took months for me to fully blossom into true motherhood. Slowly, almost too slowly to notice, over the days and nights that became weeks and then months, I evolved into a new person.

Every new mother expects her life to change with the birth of a baby, and for some women, this change is more than just an altering of their daily schedule. Your personality, your temperament, and the way you view the world around you can be transformed as well by your entry into the realm of motherhood. We cannot help but carry the lessons we learn through motherhood—patience, compassion, perseverance, creativity—into the rest of our world. Unfortunately, there are some negative emotions—frustration, anxiety, impatience—that also spill out of the nursery.

"Motherhood has made me more aggressive, more assertive, more self-assured," said Lisa. "I bought a house, had a baby, and changed jobs all in one year. Now I know I can do anything."

What motherhood hasn't done, she said, is make her a nicer person. "I just don't have much patience anymore. My life has to be very structured. I'm definitely bitchier now."

My own capacity for tolerance has both increased and decreased during the year. I find that I must use so much patience with Jesse that I have very little left for anybody else without consciously making a considerable effort. I used to be the "Dear Abby" for all my friends and an occasional stranger, but I am less generous with my time now. I grow impatient with friends who can never seem to get to the point, and I am not as good a listener as I once was. This is probably because a corner of my mind is always thinking about Jesse, even (or maybe especially) when he is not with me.

Anne, on the other hand, said her new role as a mother has made her more patient and compassionate with others and has instilled her with an instinct to nurture. She said motherhood has changed "the person inside" as much as it has changed her lifestyle.

"Before Tori was born, I was very much into myself, what I needed and wanted. Now I am concerned with the world around me, much more sympathetic, more empathetic with others."

The responsibility of parenting is a great motivator for self-awareness. It forces us to reexamine our beliefs and our values and to take a position on issues that may have held little interest for us before. I have always been fairly liberal on social and economic issues, but I have detected a growing conservatism to my nature in recent months and a greater concern over family values and education. I shocked myself one evening by actually nodding in agreement with a comment by Rush Limbaugh.

"Gun control has become a passionate issue for me since my daughter was born," Anne said. "I hate guns, and I want them all banned. I have always considered myself very conservative politically. That's how I was raised. My parents see my stand on guns as being very liberal, and we argue about it all the time, but it has nothing to do with other people's rights. I'm just afraid that Tori might one day be hurt by a gun, and the fewer guns there are, the less danger she will be in because of them."

Other women said becoming a mother has shifted their views on such controversial social and political issues as abortion, the death penalty, and prayer in schools.

"I used to believe strongly in a woman's right to have an abortion, but now I don't know," said Patti. "Now that I'm a mother, I know I could never make that decision myself."

Just as motherhood creates new social and political platforms for us, it also may eliminate a few old priorities. New mothers often abandon many of their own interests during the early years and focus almost exclusively on the issues that affect their children. For Lisa, always an active, involved member of her community, motherhood has curtailed most of her commitments to church, social, and civic organizations.

"Until Alexis is in school, I can attend things, but no more leadership roles," Lisa said. "Motherhood has definitely taught me how to say no."

A great many activities that used to be priorities in Kelli's life also have been curtailed by the new demands of motherhood. "I didn't realize how much of my time would be consumed by our baby. There's not even time to vacuum the floor," she said. "We used to spend a lot of time and energy on our house—remodeling projects and yard work. Now we just maintain."

For Tracy, motherhood has caused a change in attitude about work. "I used to work all the time. I'm self-employed now and only work three days a week, so we have less income."

Having a baby also has instilled in her a much greater sense of caution. "I used to be more carefree. Now I am very careful in whatever I do. I don't drive as fast, and I don't go into certain neighborhoods. Life has become so much more precious."

Karen also said motherhood has changed her perspective on life. "I look at life a lot differently. There's much more to it now than my own selfish needs."

Karen said she too has become much more patient with everyone around her. "I'm a teacher, so I've always had patience, but now I seem to have more of it for my husband and others outside the classroom."

Motherhood, Jennifer said, has made her a lot more understanding and less judgmental, especially about the way other parents handle their children.

"Now, I'm the first one to open a bag while shopping at the grocery store and stuff a cookie in my kid's mouth," she said. "You do whatever you have to just to keep them happy when you're out in public."

She said being a mother has also made her more aware and more thankful of "all the little things. I know that sounds corny, but I realize now what is important and what isn't. I don't worry so much about clothes. In fact, I shop for him now and not for myself. I can't remember the last time I bought something for me."

Like Jennifer, I rarely shop for myself now, and I too have slowed down behind the wheel and rarely take the freeway if a slower-paced surface street is an option.

It was nice to learn that my own transformation from a blithe spirit into a paragon of temperance and moderation had not been so out of the ordinary. My lifestyle has been irreversibly altered and my character redefined, but overall I am happy with the person I am becoming. I do, however, miss finishing a cup of coffee while it's still hot and going to the bathroom alone.

BURIED TREASURES

When I first began to write this book, I thought perhaps it should be titled *How to Survive a Mother's First Year*. It took me a while to realize that the goal should be to enjoy the first year, not just to survive it. Those mothers who beam with pleasure whenever they talk of their children have found the real bounty of motherhood—that joy that comes from loving someone so unconditionally and having that love returned just as unequivocally.

The tool for uncovering that treasure seems largely to be attitude. If you let yourself become buried under the weight of responsibility and weariness that naturally comes with the job, you will be blind to the wealth of happiness motherhood can bring to you.

The first few months were a blur of sleepless nights, endless diaper changes, nonstop breast-feeding, and a myriad of emotional and physical adjustments. My life was in chaos with so many new things to learn and so much to worry about. It was not easy to slow down and savor the precious moments.

Motherhood did get easier as the year progressed—as my baby's schedule became more consistent, as he learned to communicate and interact with me, and as I learned to adjust my priorities. The physical and emotional demands increased the more mobile he became, but the self-confidence I gained over the year enabled me to handle the burgeoning task without it becoming an oppressive burden.

As my doctor had predicted, six months was a turning

point for me, physically and emotionally. It was not until then that I began to learn how to slow down a little, ignore the clutter, and enjoy the gift I had been given.

The first step was to let go of the need for perfect order in my life. I was driving myself nuts trying to pick up every toy that got left on the floor and sanitize every teething ring that was dropped in the dirt. I felt like I was permanently attached to the vacuum.

In time, motherhood freed me of many of my compulsions to impress people with my cooking and keep that perfect, everything-in-its-place house. It also gave me a great excuse not to iron.

"Don't beat yourself up over the little things," said Tracy, who admitted that her house "is a lot more messy" since her son was born. "At first I got so frustrated because I couldn't do it all, then I realized that the important thing was spending time with Nathan."

Most experienced mothers have a priceless mental inventory of tips on how to make the first year a happy memory instead of an unpleasant one. For the most part, their suggestions are all about attitude.

You have to set limits for yourself and accept that some jobs just won't get done, Kelli suggested. "Motherhood is much, much better than I anticipated. I want to be that perfect mom. But I am finally succumbing to the reality that I can't do everything."

New mothers cannot let themselves become stagnant, she added. A baby's world is constantly changing, and a new mother must soak up information like a sponge. Kelli said she watches other mothers all the time, strangers as well as friends and family, hoping to discover their secrets of success. "I try to educate myself as much as possible. I can only give my baby the best that I've got. Mostly, I want Jordan to be as happy to have me around when he's 13 as he is happy to be with me today."

Flexibility, Karen said, is also important. "You can't get mentally stuck to a certain routine. Babies are constantly changing, and that means their schedule and your schedule is constantly changing. If you can't accept that, you are going to be frustrated all the time."

Reading everything you can on baby care is also important, Karen said, but a new mother must remember not to panic if her child is not developing "by the book. You have to relax and listen to your baby, trust your own instincts. Let your baby teach you how to be the best mother you can be."

Another secret to not only surviving but enjoying motherhood is to be patient with yourself. Becoming a mother happens overnight, but becoming a good mother takes time. Motherhood is not a project that comes to an end. It is a continual learning process, especially during the first year, when each day and sometimes each hour brings a new development.

"Babies," Lisa said after a particularly difficult weekend with her daughter, "should come with instructions, but they don't. We need a manual to keep up with the constant changes. That's why your second and third kids turn out better. You learn on your first one."

Accept that mistakes can and will be made. Most minor parenting blunders don't have far-reaching ramifications. There are few oversights that cannot be corrected. Each day is a new one; you can start all over again. If a particular method of mothering isn't working, try something different tomorrow and keep trying until you achieve the balance you need.

New mothers, Lisa added, must not only be prepared for emergencies, they must expect them to happen. A day without at least a minor crisis will be rare. Every bump you kiss and make well, each messy diaper you change without getting your baby's feet into it, and all the times you sidestep a temper tantrum will only add to your sense of self-confidence and prowess as a mother.

From Jennifer came this advice: "Keep a very good sense of humor, and learn to laugh at the things that would have embarrassed you before. Don't worry too much about disturbing other people. Don't worry about what they think. Most of them, if they have kids, have been through it themselves."

Jennifer, you might remember, is the mom whose son made an escape during a diaper change on the floor of a restroom, popping up between the knees of a very surprised stranger seated on the toilet.

"It only gets worse when they begin to walk and talk," she said. "We were on a flight, and there was a one-armed man sitting in an aisle seat in front of us. Collin grabbed the man's sleeve, peered up into it, and said, 'Uh-oh, uh-oh.' That would have mortified me a year ago. Now I take it all in stride. Luckily, the man had a good sense of humor. He said that was the best laugh he'd had in a long time."

A good sense of humor will get you through all those moments when you don't know whether to laugh or cry. It will help you maintain some perspective amid the mayhem. Something I found to be equally beneficial is the ability to count your blessings, no matter how horrible the day has been.

Make it a habit to end each day remembering only the good things. I wish I had possessed this nugget of maternal wisdom in the early months, when I not only wondered if I would survive motherhood but often questioned whether I would make it through the day. It was not until Jesse was almost a year old that I made this a part of my daily routine: I would stand over his crib for a few minutes at bedtime, watch him drift into sleep, say a prayer to keep him safe through the dark solitude of night, and mentally list each funny, happy, tender experience we had shared that day.

This recital seemed to magically banish any feelings of stress, resentment, or exhaustion the day had left me with. It helped me to forget the temper tantrum, the broken vase, the library book with ripped pages, and the jar of peanut butter smeared across the cabinet doors and massaged into the carpet. No matter what the day had been like, I could always salvage at least one precious memory to treasure.

Sometimes it would be the look of absolute triumph on Jesse's face when he toddled over to the coffee table and claimed the coveted remote control, or the big, wet, face-sucking kiss he gave me when I picked him up at the sitter's and the sweet smile he gave me just before he fell asleep.

Then I start the next day fresh, without agonizing over the mistakes I made the day before.

When my mother was struggling with depression following my father's death, I sent her a refrigerator magnet that said, "Most folks are about as happy as they make up their minds to be." I find this to be particularly good advice for first-time mothers, too. We can let our new role overwhelm us and exhaust us, or we can choose to be cheerful and calm, taking the bad days in stride and rejoicing in the good ones.

Index